A SURFEIT OF MAGNIFICENCE

The Champneys arms, family motto, Pro patria non timidus perire
'Not afraid to die for their Country'

A SURFEIT OF MAGNIFICENCE

The Trials & Tribulations of Sir Thomas Champneys of Orchardleigh

MICK DAVIS

THE HOBNOB PRESS

First published in the United Kingdom in 2021

by The Hobnob Press,
8 Lock Warehouse,
Severn Road, Gloucester GL1 2GA
www.hobnobpress.co.uk

British Library Cataloguing in Publication Data
A catalogue record for this book is available from the British Library

ISBN 978-1-914407-06-2

Typeset in Scala 11/14 pt.

Typesetting and origination by John Chandler

CONTENTS

Acknowledgements		vi
Abbreviations and Explanations		vi
Further Research		vii
The Author		viii
1	A Somerset Town	1
2	An Inheritance of Debt	5
3	Thomas Swymmer Comes of Age	16
4	The Volunteers Dispute of 1803	30
5	Champneys v Ireland 1806-1809	43
6	Ireland V Champneys 1811-1813	55
7	1819 The Dog, The Bailiff and The Judge	64
8	1820 Kidnap and Imprisonment	79
9	Unnatural Practices? August 1820	87
10	Court and the King's Bench Rules	96
11	Messiter and Release	106
12	Jamaica, Prison and Litigation 1822-1827	113
13	1828 The George Higgins Affair	123
14	The Frome Election of 1832	127
15	The Aftermath. Taunton, March 1833	143
16	Taunton Assizes, April 1834	146
17	A Surfeit of Magnificence	153
Appendix	Shakespeare's Night in Frome?	157
	William Henry Ireland	164
Bibliography		172
Index		174

ACKNOWLEDGEMENTS

Thanks are due to Clive Wilkins for his help with research, Michael McGarvie for the loan of various documents and permission to reproduce items from his extensive library; Alastair MacLeay for reading through the draft and his comments and support, Jon Ryman of Frome Museum for searching out various items, John Isherwood for sharing his research into Penton Lodge, Dr Nicholas Courtney for his help with the Cox family and of course my wife Lorraine for her forbearance and understanding.

I am also grateful to Andy Langley the Frome Fossil who inadvertently sparked the project off with his articles in *The List*: Frome, some years ago.

ABBREVIATIONS AND EXPLANATIONS

For the sake of brevity and to avoid pages of footnotes, references to newspapers have not been included unless they are of particular importance, in which case the title is included in the text. The main publications consulted are listed in the bibliography

The following abbreviations have been used sparingly:

BC Bath Chronicle
FSLS Frome Society for Local Study
FSYB/ YB Frome Society Yearbook
HRO Hampshire Record Office
SRO Somerset Record Office
UCL University College London

FURTHER RESEARCH

The Frome Society for Local Study was founded in 1958 and now has over 400 members. There is a regular programme of lectures, coach trips and town walks as well as a stream of over 100 publications of local and historical interest including a twice-yearly news bulletin, *Contact* and an annual *Yearbook* full of articles about Frome and local villages. Membership is open to anyone with an interest in the town and surrounding area particularly those interested in its history and environment. Membership is £10 per year or £15 for couples.

We are always on the lookout for interesting articles about Frome and its environs, if you would like to contribute please contact the editor at yearbookeditor@fsls.org.uk

The Society can be contacted via its website www.fsls.org.uk or via Frome Museum 01373 454611 1 North Parade, Frome BA11 1AT

Frome Museum The town museum goes from strength to strength and has now added a brilliant on-line catalogue to its many services. It has an ever-changing series of exhibits along with its permanent displays and a fascinating 'street of shops' in its lower gallery. There is an extensive library available for research by appointment. The museum is open from mid March until mid November 10.00am till 2.00pm or by special arrangement. Entry is free but donations are always welcome.

The museum can be contacted at info@frome-heritage-museum.org or fromemuseum.wordpress.com 01373 454611. 1 North Parade Frome BA11 1AT

THE AUTHOR

Mick Davis was brought up in Plymouth and Uxbridge before spending many years with one of London's top criminal defence law firms. He first came to Frome in the late 1980s before moving down permanently in 2005.He spends his time researching and writing about Frome's history and biography. Recent publications include,

The Historic Inns of Frome, a history and guide to all the towns pubs past and present.
The Awful Killing of Sarah Watts, detailed history of Frome's unsolved murder of 1851 (with David Lassman)
Of Mounds and Men , The Prehistoric Barrows of the Frome Area.
The Adventures of a Victorian Con Woman. telling the story of Mrs Gordon Baillie one of Britain's greatest con-artists. (with David Lassman).

Mick is a member of the Frome Society for Local Study and editor of its *Yearbook.*

I
A SOMERSET TOWN

Anyone who has an interest in the history of Frome and the surrounding area will have heard the story of Sir Thomas Champneys, master of Orchardleigh, the arrogant, wastrel son of an ancient and distinguished line who dissipated the huge family fortune on high living, indulgent tastes and spurious court cases. Although this is certainly the accepted view, the truth may have been quite a bit different. One of the people to paint his life in such a bad light was John Webb Singer, the brass founder and factory owner, in an article he wrote on 'Frome Worthies' for the *Somerset Standard* in 1893, some 54 years after his subject's death.[1] Singer dates the family's downfall from around 1800, in which he is sadly mistaken as the family's problems go back much further than that.

The Champneys estates at Orchardleigh are described by John Collinson, the Somerset historian writing in 1791 as dating back to the Domesday Book where it is named as *Horcerlei,* and he spells it in his own time as *Orchardley,* a

> very small parish 1½ miles north of Frome containing only five houses and 28 inhabitants. The river Frome washes this parish on the south. The lands are in general good, much thereof being water meadow worth about £3 per acre the rest which is chiefly pasture worth an average of 26 shillings per acre'[2]

By 1801 the parish was home to only 32 people and it reached its greatest number in 1891 when it had risen to 47.

The Somerset town of Frome has a noble pedigree stretching back to the 7th century and possibly before, as recent excavations at Spring Gardens have uncovered an artefact dating from around 500AD.[3] Whatever the origins of the town there were certainly people in the area during the early Neolithic period, as we know from the now destroyed

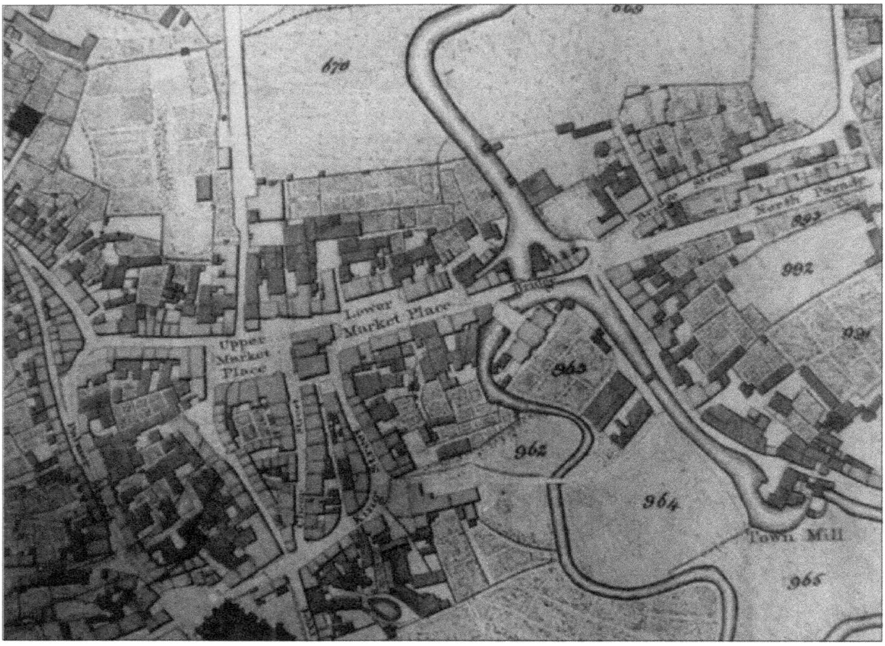

The town as Champneys would have known it in 1813 by Jeremiah Cruse

Fromefield long barrow; although the Romans do not seem to have paid much attention to the area, as little has been discovered to indicate any settlement. One of its big advantages is that it was conveniently placed for the sheep-rearing districts of the Mendip Hills and Wiltshire Downs as well as having an abundant supply of water to power the mills along the River Frome.

The period that concerns us, from the mid eighteenth century until the first decades of the nineteenth, was one of mixed fortunes. The town had risen to prominence due to the wool trade based on the production of a heavy undyed broadcloth, and after a slump in the 1630s many fortunes were made and great houses constructed on the back of a change of direction. This was due to demand for lighter coloured fabrics which led to the growth of a cloth dyeing industry, as well as various subsidiary manufactories on a large scale.[4] One of these was the growing of the woad plant (*Isatis tinctoria*), which produced a vivid blue dye used in military uniforms and other cloths, but which had the unfortunate side effect of turning its workers bright blue when they came into contact with it – 'as deeply tinged as ancient Britons', as a contemporary writer put it.[5] Alongside the wool trade there grew up a tradition of metal founding with the arrival of the Cockey family in around the 1680s, when they set up a small bell foundry which expanded over the years to a sizeable industry. There was also a substantial tradition of brewing, quarrying and many other smaller industries which supported these.

The town's reputation grew and its population along with it. Despite its grandness and prosperity, the town was a rough and lawless place in the 18th century with many pubs which brewed a strong ale to slake the thirst of its multitude of workers. The town's success drew in many undesirable characters and in 1726 there was a serious riot by the weavers, which was contained with difficulty and the ringleaders sent to Ilchester jail. There was trouble again in 1757 because of the escalating price of food instigated this time by the colliers, and followed by intermittent discontent throughout this period. The introduction of cloth production in factories with the aid of machines like the spinning jenny introduced in 1764 caused much friction, as it put the slower hand wool weavers out of work and there were many incidences of machines being smashed by the disgruntled homeworkers.

There was also much competition from the more efficient factory systems in Yorkshire. By 1785 there were at least four spinning jennies working in the town, and by 1787 shearing machines had been introduced. These reduced a great deal of homeworking and more rioting broke out despite the risk of imprisonment or even a death sentence.[6]

The Sheppard family of clothiers were among the first to build factories in Frome with a large building at Spring Gardens from about 1788. By 1833 they were employing about 2,000 people and ran four huge steam engines. As well as the clothing manufacturers there were the local dyers – Olive, Meares, Jeffries, Britton, Houston and Button.

The war with France had its effect of course as much Frome cloth had been exported there, but increased need for military uniforms soon took up the slack. The general situation had not improved by the beginning of the 19th century, which was a time of mass unemployment and poverty due in part to the introduction of machinery and competition from the northern powerhouses. They did not have the tradition of clothmaking on hand looms and therefore provoked less opposition from the indigenous workforce. The population decreased from 12,200 in 1831 to 11,279 in 1841 as people moved away to find work. One-sixth of the houses were uninhabited, properties worth £300 per year were now producing only £100, out of 271 broad and narrow looms 138 were unemployed, pawnbrokers were flourishing and other trades depressed.

This then, is just some of the background of Thomas Champneys' life; a rough and ready market town with a growing and vibrant manufacturing class, great wealth pushing aside the old aristocratic and farming traditions, causing poverty and insecurity which had its effect way beyond that of the humble worker.

[1] Reprinted in the *Frome Society Year Book*, volume 9 for 2004.
[2] Collinson, volume 2 1791
[3] YB 23 p11 The Aldefeld Francisca
[4] McGarvie 1980
[5] Richard Warner writing in 1801
[6] Goodall 2008

2

AN INHERITANCE OF DEBT

According to family tradition the Champneys family came over with the Norman invaders in 1066, the name merely indicating origins in the Champagne area of France. Exactly when and how they came to Orchardleigh is not known but probably through marriage, although the monumental tablet to Richard Champneys in the little church of St Mary at Orchardleigh describes him as 21st in descent from Sir Amian Champneys Kt., 'possessor of this place since 1131', which was certainly an exaggeration. In the late fourteenth century John de Merland, descendant of Sir Henry de Merland of Orchardleigh, a celebrated warrior and contemporary of Edward III, married Joan

St Mary's Orchardleigh in 2020

daughter of Sir John Champneys and it is thought that the Champneys of Orchardleigh are descend from her brother Sir Hugh Champneys.[1] They were established at Orchardleigh by 1431 owning much land and property in the area and deriving their income from the rents of their farms and tenements.

The suppression of the Abbey of Cirencester in 1538, which owned the living of the parish church in Frome, meant that all its lands were available for redistribution. Henry Champneys who had acquired land belonging to St Catherine's Chapel before this time now became greatly enriched. In 1660 the Champneys sold the chapel itself and the land surrounding it to John Sheppard, founder of the clothmaking firm, and Benjamin Avery, a local lawyer.[2] The oldest existing part of the estate is the church of St Mary whose origins lie in the 13th century, and which sits in the middle of an artificial lake excavated by Thomas Swymmer Champneys in around 1800. He had the church remodelled at that time in a flamboyant gothic style but it was practically rebuilt once more by Sir George Gilbert Scott during the time of the Duckworths' in 1878.

The period that seems to mark the beginnings of the family's decline, starts with Richard Champneys (1699-1761). Richard was educated at New College, Oxford and became a magistrate in 1737, but little is known about him except that he was an enthusiastic landscape gardener, whose grounds at Orchardleigh were praised by the Frome poet Samuel Bowden. Despite a large fortune of his own and marriage to two very wealthy women, he managed to accumulate debts, so large that he died being, 'indebted to divers persons by Bonds, Notes and otherwise, to a great Amount'.[3] His first wife was Sarah, daughter of Sir William Daines, a Bristol merchant and sheriff of the city in 1694 when he was knighted. He became Mayor of Bristol in 1700 and sat as its MP from 1701-1710 and again from 1714-1721, deriving his fortune from tobacco plantations in Virginia. Richard and Sarah married in 1722 and he was made Sheriff of Somerset in 1728 but does not seem to have actually served. [4] Sarah died in 1734 having produced two daughters, Elizabeth and Catherine. [5]

His heir, Thomas Champneys, was the son of his second wife, Jane Langley Swymmer, the heiress to large estates and sugar plantations along the Nutts River in Jamaica whom he married in 1739. Richard died in 1761 at his home in Fareham, Hampshire when Thomas was only 16 and still legally a minor; instructions in his will directed that the estate should be left in the care of two named trustees.

The first of these was Jane's brother and therefore Thomas's uncle, Anthony Langley Swymmer, a Bristol merchant born on the family sugar plantations in Jamaica who was at one time MP for Southampton. He died childless in January of 1760 at the age of 34 almost two years before Richard. His sugar plantations totalled over 8,000 acres and were left in trust to his nephew but the estates were incumbered with annuities, mortgages and bequests.

The other guardian was to have been Thomas Skurray, a lawyer from a large legal family based in Beckington with a practice in Bath. These two were to manage the affairs of young Thomas as his guardians until he reached full age. The trouble was that Swymmer was dead and Skurray wanted nothing to do with the matter – probably foreseeing the financial mayhem that lay ahead. A new trustee had to be appointed, and this was Elias Benjamin de la Fontaine senior, the husband of Richard's daughter Katherine Chandler Champneys – young Thomas's brother-in-law – the product of Richard's second marriage to Jane and older than him by around 20 years. Fontaine was described as a merchant of Leadenhall Street, London, and member of the Society of Spectacle Makers – which does not mean that he had anything to do with optics as anyone could join after being proposed by existing members and payment of a fee, in his case 46 shillings and 8 pence.[6] Membership meant that he became a Freeman of the City of London, which since the middle ages had given members the right to trade, or carry out their craft in the Square Mile.

There is some doubt as to how well Fontaine performed this task. When sorting out Richard's accounts Fontaine discovered that his 'personal estate was exhausted'[7] and would cover only a part of his debts. Fontaine himself appears among lists of bankrupts, firstly in 1763 and again in 1771; and many years later, after the death of his father, Thomas Swymmer put a large part of the blame for the state of the family finances at Fontaine's door. He wasn't afraid to say so, having had the memorial tablet to his father inscribed with the words

> he inherited very considerable estates from his father and uncle ... but from mismanagement by his guardians during his minority and too

easy and liberal a disposition through life no less than six entire manors with other property was alienated from the family estates.

Thomas came of age in 1766 and the following year on 26 January, he was made a baronet,

> ...in consideration of the antiquity of his family, which enjoyed such large possessions in the county of Somerset, with splendour and hospitality, for so many centuries, and of the additional fortune which he inherited by the death of his uncle Anthony Langley Swymmer, Esq; without issue; was created a baronet of Great Britain, by the name and title of Sir Thomas Champneys, of Orchadley, in the county of Somerset, Bart.[8]

The following year on July 8th he married Caroline Ann Cox the elder daughter of Richard Cox,[9] an army agent of Albemarle Street London.

Caroline Cox (Champneys) by Sir Joshua Reynolds 1764 (Heritage Auctions)

The debts and obligations left by his father, Richard were huge, amounting to some £6,500, well over a million pounds in today's money,[10] meaning that the terms of his will could not be met. In June 1770 an Act of Parliament was required to set the will aside and enable the sale of various properties, so as to release some funds to put affairs in order. Two wealthy businessmen were charged with the job. Richard Cox of Aspenden Hall, Hertfordshire (father-in-law to Sir Thomas), and Anthony Pye, an 'agent' and commissioner of bankruptcy of Featherstone Buildings, Holborn. These two were charged with selling enough property to settle the debts and obligations of Richard Champneys, with the residue paid into the Court of Chancery. Thomas also set about paying off what he could from his father's estates and even paid some debts with his own money, but despite all their efforts things were far from satisfactory.

Like his predecessors Sir Thomas held the office of Sheriff of Somerset, in the year 1775.He moved out to Jamaica briefly to run the plantations leaving his wife and children in England. Some of his account books for the years 1807-1820 survive in the Hampshire Record Office. They detail the quantities of sugar and rum he sent back to Bristol and the amount and variety of goods bought in to keep the business going, including clothing, cheese, beef, and 'best strong beer'. His accounts show that the estate just about broke even, year by year, which couldn't have helped the family finances.

His only surviving son, Thomas Swymmer Champneys, was born on 21 May 1769, and baptised at St George in Hanover Square, Westminster. He was born the heir to two generations of unpaid bills and outstanding obligations. Little has been discovered about his early years but Richard Cox his father-in-law was a friend of David Garrick the actor, who sent a note of congratulations, upon the birth of young Thomas Swymmer,

> In ye first Place as it is nearest my heart, I most Sincerely and affecty felicitate You on your Grandfathership: I beg that You will say Every thing that Yr Kindness will Suggest to Mrs Cox, the Lady in the Show, and Sr Tho Champness, for Mrs Garrick and Me.[11]

The only portrait of Thomas Swymmer known to have survived from any period is a miniature watercolour on ivory of him and his

Thomas Champneys aged 8 & sister Caroline (died 1793), painted in 1777 by Vaslet of Bath (Formerly with Ellison Fine Art)

sister Caroline by Lewis Vaslet of Bath and dating from 1777.

It seems that his early education took place locally, as there is an entry in an accounts book belonging to his mother which reads, 'To Mr Mason for Master Champneys schooling at Frome from September 1777 to December 1779 £75/4/-'.[12]

In 1780 at the age of 11[13] Thomas attended Harrow School and some of his bills still exist, including one dated from 5 February 1780 for a Dr Heath who charged £3 guineas for his entrance into Harrow. A list of general bills and invoices among the papers of the Cox family include 1781 bills from Elizabeth Arnold for board £5/5/- plus extra washing at 2/6. The school had no boarders at that time and pupils often leased lodgings from women on the hill known as 'dames', [14] presumably Mrs Arnold was the dame with whom he boarded. Greek Grammar 2/6 pens per hundred 2/3. bill inscribed 'Master Champneys debts to

French master' £3/7/6 for half years attendance, entrance and grammar exercises, and 'To John Ware for cleaning his shoes August to December 45/-.

Another rather long invoice dated from 25 September until 29 November 1781 is addressed simply to 'Master Champneys' from a Thomas Batt who was presumably a carpenter. The invoice details a variety of building works, including the construction of a pigeon house with six holes in his garden, along with works to various doors, windows and shelving. Though it is by no means clear where this was, possibly he was allowed to bring Mrs Arnold's premises up to his own exacting standards.

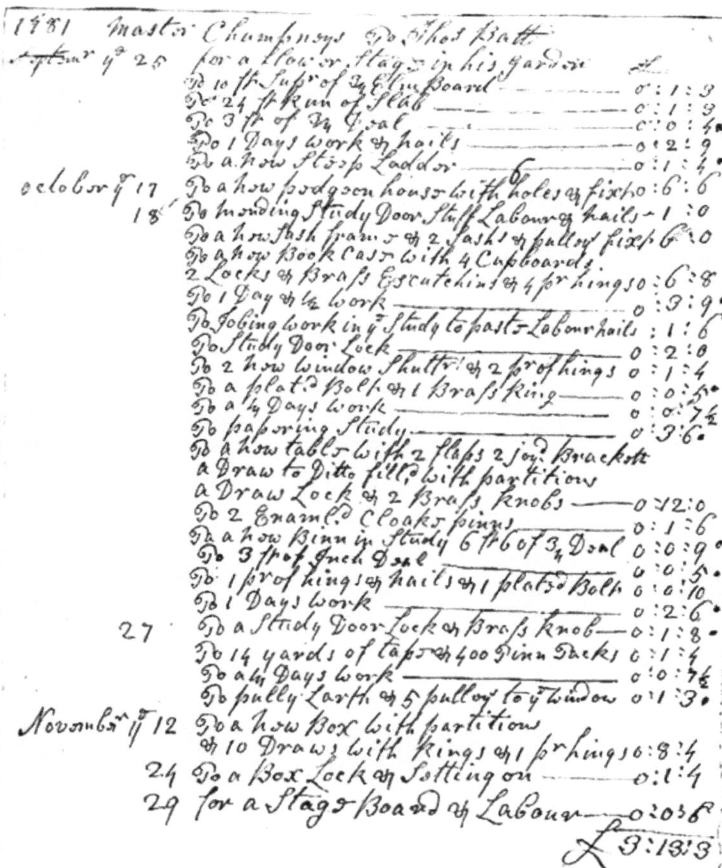
1781 Master Champneys Dr to Thos Batt
Septembr ye 25 for a flow'r stage in his garden £
To 10 ft Supr of 3/4 Elm Board — 0 : 1 : 3
Do 24 ft Run of Slab — 0 : 1 : 3
To 3 ft of 3/4 Deal — 0 : 0 : 4½
To 1 Days work & nails — 0 : 2 : 9
To a new Step Ladder — 0 : 1 : 4
October ye 17 To a new pidgeon house with 6 holes & fixing 0 : 6 : 6
18 To mending Study Door Stuff Labour & nails - 1 : 0
To a new Sash frame & 2 Sashes & pulleys fixing 6 : 0
To a new Book Case with 4 Cupboards
2 Locks & Brass Escutchins & 4 pr hinges 0 : 6 : 8
To 1 Day & ½ work — 0 : 3 : 9
To Jobing work in ye Study to paste Labour nails : 1 : 6
To Study Door Lock — 0 : 2 : 0
To 2 new window Shuttrs & 2 pr of hinges 0 : 1 : 4
To a plated Bolt & 1 Brass Ring — 0 : 0 : 5
To a ½ Days work — 0 : 0 : 7½
To papering Study — 0 : 3 : 6
To a new table with 2 flaps 2 joynd Brackets
a Draw to Ditto filled with partitions
a Draw Lock & 2 Brass knobs — 0 : 12 : 0
To 2 Enameld Cloake pinns — 0 : 1 : 6
To a new Binn in Study 6 ft 6 of 3/4 Deal 0 : 0 : 9
To 3 ft of Inch Deal 0 : 0 : 5
To 1 pr of hinges & nails & 1 plated Bolt 0 : 0 : 10
To 1 Days work — 0 : 2 : 6
27 To a Study Door Lock & Brass knob — 0 : 1 : 8
To 14 yards of tape & 400 Pinn Tacks 0 : 1 : 4
To a ½ Days work — 0 : 0 : 7½
To pully Larth & 5 pulleys to ye window 0 : 1 : 3
Novembr ye 12 To a new Box with partitions
& 10 Draws with Rings & 1 pr hinges 0 : 8 : 4
24 To a Box Lock & Setting on — 0 : 1 : 4
29 for a Stage Board & Labour — 0 : 0 : 6
£ 3 : 13 : 3

Carpentry work to Champney's lodgings at Harrow (M McGarvie)

After leaving Harrow he went to Winchester College like his father before him, and college records indicate that he was there during 1783-84 as a 'commoner' or fee payer when he would have been 14 years old. Mrs Champneys records in her accounts book that the entrance fee was £9/16/06. These boys were very much the private pupils of the headmaster which means that they have left little mark in the official school records. It was quite usual for boys to be at the school for such a short time, about a year in this case, especially the commoners, but there was no legal requirement for children to be in education and so it was entirely up to the parents as to whether a child was sent to school and for how long, and it is highly likely that money for school fees became an issue in this case.

By 1785 Sir Thomas's debts had become so bad that in June he was ordered by the High Court of Chancery to sell various 'parcels of land, tenements, and messages' in several lots which were leased to various tenants; the purchaser of course was entitled to the rents, reducing their income still further. Documents in the Somerset Record Office relate to the deeds of a number of properties being sold off in 1817 and 1820 including Whatcombe Farm, Lullington Farm, Jeffries Mill and some of the inherited Swymmer land in Jamaica.[15]

In 1787 a meeting was called at the Waggon and Horses in Frome for those owed money by Sir Thomas to discuss how best to recover some of the interest on what they were due. Whether these debts were due to the family's personal failings, those of the administrators, failed business ventures or other external pressures is not known. It was often the case that those inheriting large estates in foreign lands lacked the drive and enthusiasm of the original pioneers and left things to managers and overseers with predictable results, Sir Thomas's personal involvement does not seem to have helped much, as the plantations are not shown as bringing in money. In 1789 another large amount of land and farms around Orchardleigh were sold off by order of Chancery to pay some more of Sir Richard's debts.[16]

In 1789 at the age of 20 he was appointed a 'Gentleman of his Majesties Chapel Royal', not a building but a distinct body of priests and lay singers who 'support the spiritual needs of the monarch'. In Champneys case this would presumably have involved being part of a choir at St. James Palace.

His mother died in 1791 at Rameau near Calais in France where she had gone to recover her health but expired after a 'tedious illness'. Sir Thomas retired to his home in Exton, Hampshire where he died on 2 July 1821 and was hastily interred in the local church, much to the disgust of his son who had his remains brought back to the family vault at St Mary's Church Orchardleigh in 1822. The inscription on his tomb tells an interesting tale: -

> SIR Thomas Champneys BARONET. To the family vault of a long line of ancestors within this chapel from the parish church of Exton, in Hampshire, wherein they had been inconsiderately deposited by order of his executors. The late baronet was the only surviving son of Richard Chaundler Champneys, by Jane Swymmer his second wife, eventually sole heiress to her brother Anthony Langley Swymmer of Mold in the county of Flint, and Nutts River, in the island of Jamaica. Sir Thomas married early in life, Caroline Ann, elder daughter of Richard Cox, Esq. of Quarely House in Hampshire, by Caroline 3rd daughter of Sir William Codrington of Dodington Park in Gloucestershire, by whom he had six children, one alone surviving him: the present baronet Thomas SWYMMER Champneys, of this place.
>
> The late Sir Thomas served the office of High Sheriff for the county with great splendour in the year 1775. Was a magistrate and deputy lieutenant of the same, he inherited very considerable estates from his father and uncle in the several counties of Somerset, Hants, Wilts. Flint and Gloster, but from mismanagement by his guardians during his minority and too easy and liberal a disposition through life no less than six entire manors with other property was alienated from the family estates and Manors of Orchardleigh and Frome Selwood, and certain estates attached thereto alone remained with the plantations in Jamaica at his decease. To record a possession in the same name and family in regular descent from the Norman Conquest to the present time.
>
> Sir Thomas Departed this life at his residence in Exton, after a most severe and protracted illness of some years duration. July 2nd 1821. AGED 76
>
> Requiescat in pace (on scroll).

[1] The Marland Family – internet

[2] Belham.1985 *The Making of Frome* p 57

[3] *An Act for sale of part of the settled estates, late of Richard Champneys Esquire deceased, for payment of his debts and legacies and for other purposes therein mentioned* Frome Museum D 8350

[4] M.McGarvie notes

[5] Ancestry Hicks-Beach site

[6] An *Act for sale of part of the settled estates* ... p 3

[7] ibid

[8] *The Baronetage of England*, by Thomas Wotton.
[9] Richard Cox 1718-1803
[10] UK Inflation Calculator
[11] Nicholas Courtney unpublished manuscript
[12] Cox family papers Box 11 M. McGarvie
[13] Harrow School records.
[14] Jones, 1969
[15] SRO DD\BR\nw/13
[16] Orchardleigh Estate papers Frome Museum D415

3
THOMAS SWYMMER COMES OF AGE, 1790–1803

On 31 May 1790 young Thomas Swymmer 'came of age', it being his 21st birthday and 'upon which occasion the principle inns of the town in Mold in Flintshire (where his father Sir Thomas was Lord of the Manor) were, thrown open and very elegant entertainments provided for his friends and numerous tenants'.

As was common at that age amongst those with money and breeding Thomas seems to have embarked upon what became known as the 'grand tour' whereby young gentlemen travelled through Europe in search of art and classical culture accompanied by an older guide or chaperone. He left no details of his travels but there are two versions of a charming story dating from this period which are worth repeating as we have so little from his early years. In 1790 Thomas arrived at the court

Penton Lodge and Park from an old print

of King Frederick of Prussia in Berlin and was presented with a large poodle named Azor meaning 'mighty' or 'heroic'. The dog returned to England with his new master and became his constant companion.

In 1791 he bought Penton Lodge, Penton Mewsey just a few miles from his father who was living at Amport, and possibly he had received some money from his father's estate upon reaching his majority. It seems that he had grand plans for the house and was soon in debt and having to re-mortgage the lodge for £2,024. The mortgage deed of 1794 states that,

> The said Thomas Swymmer Champneys hath made great additions and improvements to the said Dwelling House and on part of the said premises hath lately erected Stables, Coach Houses, Offices and other buildings and hath made Gardens, Plantations, Planted Walks and other alterations and improvements...

260 Thomas Swymmer Champneys Esq. and Charlotte Margaret Mostyn both of this Parish were married in this Church by Licence this twenty first Day of April in the Year 1792 by me Thomas Mostyn [illegible]
This Marriage was solemnized between us { Thomas Swymmer Champneys / Charlotte Margaret Mostyn
In the presence of { Francis Mostyn [illegible] / Richd. Cox / [illegible]

The marriage of Thomas Champneys to Charlotte Mostyn, Hanover Sq. 21 April 1792

On 21 April 1792 Thomas married Charlotte Margaret Mostyn aged 24 at St George's Church, Hanover Square, London. Both were described as 'of that parish'; from which we can assume that he was living in London at the time. Charlotte was the second daughter of Sir Roger Mostyn, a baronet from an old and wealthy family in Flintshire. How or by whom the marriage was organised is unknown; arrangements of this type were by no means love matches but business arrangements negotiated between men and often involving significant transfers of property with lawyers involved more than the clergy. Amongst the witnesses was Richard Cox, whose family appear later in the story.

According to Frome historian J O Lewis writing in 1935 Thomas Swymmer acquired the Orchardleigh estate by indentures of lease and release dated 1st and 2nd November 1792, and by an exemplification of recovery from his father, and the married pair moved in despite it being heavily mortgaged. Undeterred he borrowed yet more money on the property which he spent very rapidly. In 1795 Champneys put the Lodge up for sale and the sales particulars list, '...an entrance hall, an inner hall which includes the main staircase, a drawing room with four windows, a dining room with three, east and west libraries, a study, a housekeeper's room, servants' hall, butler's pantry, kitchen, pantry, larder, scullery, laundry, wash and bake houses.' On the first floor were eleven bedrooms, two with dressing rooms and a school room. There were sixteen attics, including a housemaid's closet, a china closet and two lumber rooms. Outside was 'a spacious lawn, shrubberies and plantations. Stabling in the form of a crescent 94 feet in diameter (this was immediately adjoining the White Hart Inn) for 20 horses, 8 coach houses etc. A 'Beautiful Hermitage' was also included. There were also a detached farmyard, barns, granary and other buildings. These were almost certainly those which went with Manor Farm, formerly sited in the paddock to the present Penton Manor, opposite the White Hart. Finally offered for sale were '130 acres of excellent land Watered and Refreshed by a beautiful stream which runs at the bottom of it.[2]

The couple moved into Orchardleigh, which raises the interesting question of who had been occupying the mansion for the previous few years with both father and grandfather preferring Hampshire or London.

Wherever Thomas Swymmer went celebrations followed and at one of his early balls at Orchardleigh on 31 December 1796, the artist Samuel Woodforde (1763-1817), nephew to the diarist James Woodforde, was commissioned to paint some portraits, as he described in his diary entry,

> A letter for Miss Woodforde from her brother Samuel then at Thomas Champneys at his seat at Orcherly near Frome in Somerset, giving her some description of a late masquerade ball given at the house, upwards of 150 genteel people at it. It was said on the papers that it was of the first degree of taste. Samuel was at it, being there to paint some portraits.[3]

In 1797 Azor died and was buried in the grounds at Orchardleigh where a classical monument with an urn and carved dog skulls was raised over his grave. The edifice once bore the inscription:

In Memory of Azor

A Prussian by birth, and for many years the constant Companion and
Fellow Traveller of the owner of this Place.
He died April 15, 1797
Adieu! Most faithful of a faithful kind;
Though void of reason, and denied a mind:
How many a two – legged animal we see
Who boast of both and yet might copy thee.
Thy sense so prompt to catch the tricks of art,
Thy cheerful manners and thy gentle heart'
Their charms in memory so strongly blend,
"I better could have spared a better friend"
Could matchless worth prolong a mortal date,
This stone would ne'er have rehearsed thy mournful fate;
But sad experience bids me sigh and say,
Azor! like thee, "Each dog must have his day"[4]

This touching but simple story has been the subject of great elaboration over the years and is worth a small diversion. There is another version which states that Thomas was rescued from drowning off the coast of Denmark by a large and skilful dog and that when he died his bones were interred within St Mary's Church. Given Thomas's love of display and drama, if this was what had actually happened then surely it would have formed part of the inscription.

This was the version, however that was taken up and expanded upon by the Rev John B. Medley in the late 1870s, who claims that the dog's bones were found inside the church in the Champneys' chapel. He also claimed that the inscription stated that he had lost his 'truest friend', which upset his wife Charlotte so much that she retired alone to Wales for six weeks. Medley was probably confused by an almost identical tale recorded in the 1838 diary of local philanthropist Tom Bunn,[5] who says that he once saw a monument to a dog made from Coade Stone. It told the tale of a gentleman who was bathing in the sea and got out of his depth, when a fine Newfoundland dog sprang from a nearby vessel and assisted him to the shore. He was a man of fortune and, conscious that he owed his life to this dog, purchased it and ordered a tomb to be constructed in his park upon its death. Bunn did not mention names or the location of the monument.

Azor's monument in St. Mary's church

The Victorian poet Sir Henry Newbolt was inspired by the story, which he came across whilst courting Margaret Duckworth, daughter of the estate's new owners, and in 1898 he wrote a poem entitled *Fidele's*

Grassy Tomb, taking many liberties with the facts but producing an amusing work.

In 1831 upon the death of her brother, Sir Thomas Mostyn, the majority of his estates went to Charlotte and thus to Thomas, who was granted permission to add the arms of the Mostyn family quarterly to his own, and to add the family name to his own becoming Sir Thomas Swymmer Mostyn-Champneys. His sister Caroline died in Lisbon in 1793, at the age of 21 where she had gone to 'recover her health'. Her memorial in St Mary's church includes a marble plaque showing a woman resting her elbow on a pillar.

> (Signed "King and Son Londini fecit"). In affectionate remembrance of CAROLINE CHAMPNEYS eldest daughter of SIR THOMAS CHAMPNEYS BART, and DAME CAROLINE ANN his Wife, who closed a life replete with every virtue and was here buried April 28 1793. Her remains were conveyed from Lisbon, where she died in the 22nd year of her Age. Yet shall not her belov'd remembrance sleep Within the dark cold bosom of the Earth, Be ours her transient date of Life to weep. But hers to triumph in unfading worth. Which when mortality's frail scene is o'er And this vast universe shall fade away, Will place her where pale anguish groans no more Mid the bright mansions of Eternal Day.

Despite the long pedigree and the assets by marriage of several families Thomas Swymmer seemed as hopeless at dealing with the debt as his forbears, spending recklessly on vanity projects like digging the huge lake on his estate in about 1800 and extravagant balls. On one occasion it is said that Lord Cork was present at a dinner in which a live bird or animal was placed under all the dish covers of the first course to create some excitement. The *Bath Chronicle* describes the attractions at a ball to celebrate Christmas in 1798 (overleaf).

1798 was also the year in which he became one of the Sheriffs of Somerset and engaged a body of 24 javelin men, equipped and armed with a retinue for official functions. Thomas was very proud of his appointment, which had been fulfilled by his father in 1775 and his grandfather in 1728; he carried out his duties with his usual flair. Edmund Crocker, the son of Abraham Crocker the land surveyor, describes one of the processions in his diary: [6]

March 26 1800
TS Champneys having been chosen Sheriff for this county, about a dozen young men of this town ...offered their services as javelin men. They rode off this morning for Taunton (the Assizes being held there) in their common cloaths, their javelin dress etc. having been sent before in waggons to be kept smooth, dry and from spoiling.

An elegant Maſqued Ball was given by Thomas Champneys, eſq; at Orchardleigh-Houſe, on Thurſday. The different apartments were decorated with tranſparencies, artificial flowers, painted floors, &c. The Company of the firſt faſhion and reſpectability, 200 in number; the wines and ſupper ſubſtantially elegant, and many of the characters admirably ſupported; particularly, a Showman with a Fantoccini, a Mountebank Doctor with ſuperior wit and vivacity, Buonaparte leading four Friars in chains, a Doctor Pauglofs, ſeveral good ſailors, a Town-Cryer, a beautiful Ariel with a harp, a capital Wowſki, an old Swiſs with an organ, and two elegant little Savoyards, together with many others equally excellent.---Above all ſhone the Lady of the Manſion in beauty and affable politeneſs.——The company did not ſeparate till ſeven o'clock, when 18 carriages filled with maſks returned to Bath.

A masked ball at Orchardleigh from the Bath Chronicle December 27 1798

In May 1800 the papers were full of a possible double assassination attempt on the life of George III. While he was reviewing some troops in Hyde Park a shot was fired, narrowly missing him. Later press reports claimed that the shot was an accident and certainly no one was arrested for it. With admirable coolness his majesty continued with his itinerary and attended the theatre at Drury Lane where another shot was fired at him as the band were playing the national anthem. The shot missed and an ex-soldier named James Hadfield was arrested. He was put on trial for high treason but judged insane, saying that he wished the king no harm but wanted to end his own life and lacked the courage to do so himself. Hadfield had suffered several sabre cuts to the head while fighting the French and was almost certainly affected by the inhalation of mercury vapours while working as a silversmith. A verdict of insanity would normally have resulted in his release but on this occasion the court ordered that he be detained 'at His Majesty's Pleasure', the first time that such an order was made.

Thomas, in his capacity as sheriff, organised the issue of an address to his majesty to celebrate his escape from injury. Such meetings were held in many towns across the country and resulted in short statements in which local notables expressed their horror and wished his majesty's sacred person well. The statement that Thomas and his fellows put out with Lord Glastonbury in the chair was, for once, okay and mercifully short,

> To The King's Most Excellent Majesty
> The humble ADDRESS of the Nobility, Gentry Clergy, freeholders and other inhabitants of the COUNTY OF SOMERSET;
>
> We your Majesty's most dutiful and loyal subjects the Nobility, Gentry, Clergy and Freeholders of the County of Somerset and other inhabitants of the county of Somerset humbly beg leave to express our unanimous abhorrence of the late treasonable attempt against your Majesty's sacred person and offer our sincere congratulations on your majesties providential escape.
>
> The more we reflect only incalculable blessings we enjoy on your majesties Government the more fervent are our prayers to the Almighty to protect a life so justly dear to all your majesties subjects.
> By order of the meeting it was resolved that thanks be given to the chairman for so ably representing the sheriff in his unavoidable absence.
>
> May 26, 1800

Crocker gives details of another procession to the Assize court on 16 August 1800:

> This morning at 7.00 o'clock the javelin men proceeded to Orchardleigh to breakfast. At 10 o'clock the bells were set ringing and the procession through the town to Wells Assizes began. The state coach and six horses, with the sheriff and J.A. Wickham Esq six outriders, two clergymen and

> two trumpeters. The captain, Mr Jefferies and all the javelin men, with a numerous concourse of spectators who were not waiting long ere they were in sight. The day was remarkably fine and hot'.

~~~

DESPITE HIS FINANCIAL problems Thomas continued in his assumed role as a leader of fashionable society; he was the host of increasingly elaborate balls at Orchardleigh and a regular attendee at the most fashionable venues in London. It was a closed and elite group and he was in his element; his natural eloquence and flamboyance as well as his understanding of the social conventions and manners required would have put him at the top of any list of invitations. His eccentricities and sometimes outrageous reputation would have been appreciated and it was even rumoured that he had installed a 'lady friend' in a cottage on the Orchardleigh estate, although nothing was produced to substantiate this.[7]

On 1 January 1801 an elegant suite of apartments was thrown open at Orchardleigh to over 200 guests in his latest masquerade at which 'to heighten the hilarity of the occasion all dominoes were excluded'. The domino was a mere cloak with a plain mask which covered the upper part of the face – far too boring, unlike some of the characters, which included,

> a Jeffery Wild-Goose in search of his daughter, an Owl, a lame fiddler, Punch, a most beautiful figure in the dress of a Christ Hospital boy, a Fury clothed in the terrors of infernal paraphernalia pursuing Orestes, two chattering barbers, a dancing bear, a pretty milk maid, and a French tailor galloping on a very magnificent goose.

The article concluded, perhaps with some sarcasm, that, 'The supper was served in the richest profusion but from a laudable attention to the severity of "existing circumstances" the use of bread was entirely prohibited'.

At the beginning of June 1801, a Mrs Walker held her masquerade. The lady who cut such a distinguished figure in the fashionable life of London was the wife of a Liverpool merchant, and she was said to have been in receipt of £10,000 per annum from her husband. Tickets
~~~

were said to be available on the black market for 25 to 30 guineas. The Prince of Wales was in attendance along with an estimated 700 people. Champneys seems to have surpassed himself on this occasion. He dressed initially as Judge Ashurst but later in the evening assumed the role, in a surreal piece of theatre entitled, 'Alderman and Mrs Gobble', 'playing both persons back to back as a ludicrous emblem of the perfect conjugal union'.

DUET FOR ONE

The Alderman: -
All ye who pass wedlock in distance and strife,
Learn how close are the bonds which should join man and wife;
If you wish perfect conjugal union to see,
Behold it in dear Mrs Gobble and me!

Mrs Gobble: -
My love for my Gobble, none here can attack,
For I never quit his side-I mean quit his back!
And many wives here sure may envy my case,
Tho' in close tete-a-tete, yet I ne'er see his face,

The Alderman: -
Let the ill- married world at our happiness wonder,
And cursed be the hand that would tear us asunder;
Tho' still turning our backs on each other you've seen us,
Believe me, good folks, there is no coolness between us.

Mrs Gobble: -
Ye ladies and lords, who on Hymen's laws trample,
Attend all to mine and my Deary's example;
A connection like ours would your quarrels all smother,
If each were like us, the true half of each other.

You probably had to have been there.

In all probability the gatherings at Orchardleigh included Peter Thellusson, later 1st Baron Rendlesham of the London banking family, and his wife Elizabeth. Thellusson was born in the same year as Champneys and also attended Harrow school, which is possibly how they met. They lived in much splendour at Foley House in what is now Portland Place, and in May of 1802 they hosted a ball there to celebrate the 64th birthday of King George. Invitations were sent only to people who had invited the Thellussons to similar events on previous occasions, and the star of the show was George, Prince of Wales, who arrived with 20 followers dressed as a 'baron of ancient times in scarlet and gold'; his party dined in a supper room set aside for them. 'This party for nearly one hour supported a constant succession of mirth and good humour and although many of them early in the evening had exerted themselves in other characters particularly with Mr Champneys as an old Welshwoman on horseback with butter and eggs to market, wit and repartee did not slacken'.

Champneys' act was described as the most humorous of all and it is not hard to see how this piece of performance art would have stood out amongst the usual Highlanders, Jews, old maids, slaves and hermits. For some reason later in the evening he ended up as Dr Galen the Roman philosopher and 'father of medicine'. Mrs Champneys was described as a very beautiful woman and Prince William of Gloucester appeared in a plane domino. Mrs FitzHerbert, companion to the future George IV, was in highland dress.

In 1802 the Duke of York, Lord and Lady Bathurst, Lord Malmesbury and family, Lord and Lady John Thynne, the right honourable William Pitt, Mr and Mrs Champneys and Sir Richard Hoare attended a shooting party at the Marquis of Bath's Longleat estate in Wiltshire, and at the beginning of February 1803 the Champneys gave a grand masquerade at Orchardleigh followed by a ball and supper. It seems that Thomas and Caroline were spending most of their time in London, leading a life of fun and frivolity amongst those slightly above their station in life and certainly above their income. In May of that year Lady Louisa Manners held her first 'assembly' at her splendid mansion in Pall Mall as the very elegant leader of the *'haut ton'* or high fashion amongst the elite of Georgian society. They exhibited the high tone and refined manners which characterised those of good breeding and fortune, representing that part of society that was able to live in luxury and spend a large amount of their time pursuing pleasure; families with rank, connections and wealth. A short time later the Countess of Mount-Norris held a masked ball at the earl's magnificent villa at Ealing Grove for 400 people of the first rank of society; admission was by ticket only and Lord Mount-Norris examined the tickets himself to look for forgeries. The Prince of Wales arrived at 11pm, Mr Champneys appeared as a countryman.

Having enjoyed the many festivities slightly in advance of the king's 65th birthday there was more to come on the actual day, 6 June 1803, at the royal residence, St James Palace. The report and descriptions of those attending took up almost three pages of the London paper, the *Morning Post,* sometimes known as the *Fawning Post* because of its love of royalty and the upper classes, which included detailed descriptions of what everyone was wearing. The king was described as 'plainly dressed as usual on his own birthday while the Prince of Wales chose a Field Marshall's uniform'. Mr Thomas Champneys wore, 'A dark fine cloth coat and breeches lined with garter blue silk and an elegant silk embroidered waistcoat in silver and shades of silk', while Mrs Champneys wore a 'Dark crepe body and train with a petticoat of the same adorned with silver chains etc'. The fabulously rich Wiltshire socialite and connoisseur William Beckford was there and twelve other dinners, balls, routs and suppers took place in central London on the same evening.

In November 1803 to celebrate Christmas 40 poor families were invited from the town and villages of Frome to the 'comfort and relief 'of Orchardleigh. A couple of months later in February the real fun began. '

> A temporary ballroom had been built 60 feet in length and 50 feet across. The room was decorated by Mr Charles Davis a painter of Bath to represent an extensive grove of foreign trees and plants terminated by the Temple of Harmony to which the company passed under lofty arches of artificial flowers illuminated by a variety of lights. One band of music encouraged the light fantastic while another of more martial sounds was placed in the gallery on the staircase. From 9 to 12 o'clock the motley crew, 250 in number, assembled and a scene of more wit versatility and good humour has seldom occurred. Several characters being supported with genuine spirit and real talent among which number the hospitable donor shone conspicuous, as did his lady for elegance of dress and dignity of mien.

In case anyone had missed it previously, Champneys revised his role from the London scene as 'An Old Welshwoman going with butter and eggs to market' but this time mounted on a goat. He also did a turn as 'All the World and his Wife' which could possibly have been the double-sided costume from Mrs Gobble of a couple of years before. Mrs Champneys was dressed as a modern Parisienne. The company included a large number of the local rich and aristocratic, and among the most notable names invited were, The Marquis and Marchioness of Bath, The Earl and Countess of Cork, Viscountess Hawarden, Lady A'Court, Lady Cope, Lord Stuart, Mr Jolliffe of Ammerdown, Lady Gore, Lord Mountjoy, Sir J Hippisley, Lord Strangford, The Hon Mr Maude, Sir W Guise, Sir John Hawkins and Lady Ridley.

> From 1 to 3 o'clock the company partook of supper particularly well suited to the occasion as it contained a profusion of hot soups, game, house lamb, turkeys etc served with abundant and substantial elegance accompanied by the properly judged distinction of the single appendage of Port and Madeira wines only. Immediately after this was a ball which lasted until 7 o'clock and continued in excellent spirit, when the company departed in nearly 50 carriages well pleased with every part of the evenings amusements and 'the night being very fine the town was quite alive till 5 o'clock in the morning.
>
> Some part of the evenings amusement we understand, which was to have extended to brilliant illumination of the house without and a grand display of fireworks was prevented by the interruption of so many of the neighbouring populous crowding around the outside of the house and satisfying their idle curiosity by impeding all plausible approach to the windows and continuing, notwithstanding the coldness of the night, with open mouth and vacant stare till morning dawn.

While the balls and fashionable gatherings doubtless occupied a lot of his time there were more serious matters to be attended to.

[1] John Isherwood lecture notes
[2] ibid
[3] Woodforde p 540
[4] *The Mystery of Fidele*, FSLS 1999

[5] Lewis 1935 BC
[6] *A Journal of Remarkable Occurrences in Frome* Edmund Crocker and YB 8 p.8
[7] Batten Pooll *A West Country Pot Pourri* 1969

4
THE VOLUNTEERS DISPUTE OF 1803[1]

DURING THE NAPOLEONIC War bodies of men had been assembled to counter any possible invasion, a prototype home guard, as, without conscription, the government had little choice but to rely on the patriotism of the people through a volunteer movement whose function would be to conduct guerrilla warfare against the French occupying forces. They would operate in small bodies to harass, instil panic and wear out the French invaders. They were never expected to get deeply engaged with French troops and to retire when hard pressed. As a bit of a bonus they were also to be used as a force for the suppression of revolutionary and seditious movements at home, including having to deal with riots and disturbances of the disaffected poor.[2]

Their local knowledge was invaluable and to be used as much as possible; they were also expected to cut off French pillaging detachments. A body of men had been formed into the 'Frome Selwood Troop of Volunteer Cavalry' by Frome solicitor James Anthony Wickham (1796-1854) at the height of the threat during March 1797. Amongst their number was a Nathaniel Messiter, banker and wool stapler who is to appear later in the story. As their captain, and following an official directive, Wickham stood them down as the threat diminished with the Peace of Amiens in June 1802.

When the treaty collapsed in May of 1803, and a renewal of the threat to Great Britain by Napoleon's army was once more a possibility, there was an appeal to re-form the troops. The response was overwhelming and resulted in a mobilization of the population on a scale not previously seen in Britain, culminating in a combined military force of over 615,000 by December of that year.

Thomas Champneys Esq received his commission on 13 August

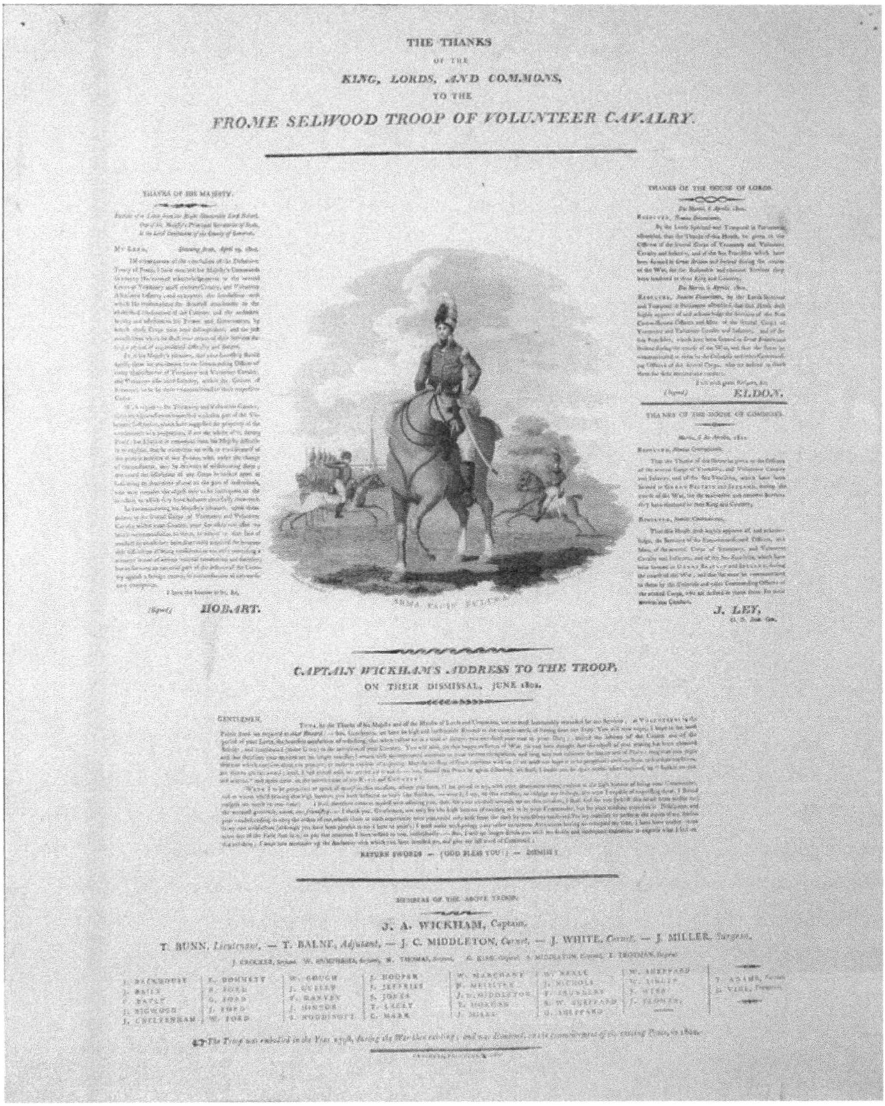
THE THANKS
OF THE
KING, LORDS, AND COMMONS,
TO THE
FROME SELWOOD TROOP OF VOLUNTEER CAVALRY.

THANKS OF HIS MAJESTY.

(Signed) HOBART.

THANKS OF THE HOUSE OF LORDS.

(Signed) ELDON.

THANKS OF THE HOUSE OF COMMONS.

J. LEY,

CAPTAIN WICKHAM'S ADDRESS TO THE TROOP,
ON THEIR DISMISSAL, JUNE 1802.

GENTLEMEN,

RETURN SWORDS — (GOD BLESS YOU!) — DISMISS!

MEMBERS OF THE ABOVE TROOP.

J. A. WICKHAM, Captain.

T. BUNN, Lieutenant, — T. BALNE, Adjutant, — J. C. MIDDLETON, Cornet, — J. WHITE, Cornet, — J. MILLER, Surgeon.

Dismissal of the Frome Troop June 1802

1802[3] and soon raised a body of volunteers totalling 500 men formed into two troops of cavalry and four companies of infantry. They were 'composed entirely of persons of property and respectability and officered by the gentlemen around them, all of whom will act free of any expense to government'. Despite his polite protestations and insistence that there were others more suitable and 'competent in military knowledge than myself' Champneys was placed in control and became Lt. Colonel of the regiment known as the Selwood Forest Legion. In July of 1803 he received a deputation which delivered a document signed by 127 'respectable inhabitants of Frome':

> FROME INFANTRY
> We the undersigned members, who intend to compose part of the Frome Infantry actuated from the very high sense we entertain of your public zeal and spirit, beg to signify our united approbation of the choice of YOU to take the command.
>
> Should you countenance this, our most ardent wish, we should be no less sensible of the importance of subordination and discipline, necessary to the establishment and support of its reputation as soldiers than in submitting to those regulations which their commander may enforce.
>
> We trust that having been thus early in our application, The Loyal Frome Volunteer Infantry may claim a preference to similar solicitations which may probably soon offer, of the same nature'.

The infantry consisted of one company at Beckington and three at Frome, and initially things went well. The men were drilled and inspected at Orchardleigh by Lt Colonel Power who expressed himself very pleased by the military appearance and performance of their manoeuvres. Everything had the blessing of the Lt. General commanding the district, John Poulett otherwise the 4th Earl Poulett (1756-1819) of Hinton St George and Lord Lieutenant of Somerset. Everything seemed to go smoothly enough, with the Frome companies happily accepting that Beckington had precedence and the various parties dining together at a Frome inn with a convivial atmosphere. Amongst those in Frome of the class considered suitable as officer material the following names where proposed and accepted.

Henry, George and William Sheppard, clothiers
John and Edward Olive, dyers
Mr James Slade, clothier of Welshmill
Mr John King, carpenter

Mr John Middleton, son to the London carrier
Mr Thomas Jones, postmaster

According to Champneys' version of events, which is the only one we have, on 6 October 1803 a meeting of the Frome infantry was held at the Crown Inn, Frome Market Place, where it was unanimously agreed that a fourth company should be formed with William Sheppard as major in command. Champneys knew nothing of this and was informed of the decision by letter. William Sheppard was the main protagonist supported by his younger brothers Henry and George, owners of the local clothing factory. At that time William held the rank of captain and was later described as 'an unpleasant and quarrelsome man who was certainly responsible for the fracas that ensued'.[4] His attitude to those with whom he disagreed is perhaps illustrated in a letter from Sheppard to a Mr Grant his tenant at Freeze Farm. Grant wanted to erect some hutches which Sheppard objected to in the following terms, '...if you persist in putting in the hutches you will find me a most hostile enemy; I will spare no expense and make you repent the day you made me resort to legal measures, which I'll pursue with energy'.[5]

The volunteers dispute developed into a matter of great personal animosity. There did not seem to have been any bad feeling between the parties before and it was probably a matter of personal ambition on the part of the Sheppard family, or it could have been simply a matter of new money against old. There does not seem to have been any problem with the forming of a new company as there were plenty of volunteers; the argument centred around the question of whether Beckington or Frome should have precedence and who should take up the various positions of command. Tradition dictated that the first company to be formed should have this right and that was Beckington. Its rank and file members were quite adamant that this should be so and this was the view that Champneys supported. He also had his own nominees for officers.

The Sheppard faction proposed that as Frome had had a distinguished record from the past war it should have precedence over what they described as 'a new company raised in a hamlet'. The recommendations were set before Poulett who replied that the first formed company would normally have precedence and that this was

Beckington, but if this could not be agreed then, 'I can therefore only recommend the mode usually practiced by which regiments fixed precedents, namely by casting lots'.

Things deteriorated and feelings ran so high in the ranks that it became unsafe for Frome and Beckington to be on parade at the same time and Poulett was frequently asked to mediate between the two. He upheld a complaint by Champneys that William Sheppard had behaved in so a disgraceful manner, and that his conduct could be described as 'very extraordinary', and that his language was so bad that it should be reported. He further suggested that Champneys withhold the armaments that were to be issued until matters between them could be resolved. 195 pikes were therefore safely stowed away in the church at Orchardleigh; the muskets and sabres had yet to arrive from the stores in Plymouth.

Poulett attempted to get the two sides to meet and discuss things with him and invited them down to Sidmouth where he was confined with the gout. Champneys was outraged that a man in his position should be asked to make the journey of 100 miles to discuss something which was to him a foregone conclusion and refused. Sheppard and his party made the journey alone and of course had the ear of his lordship.

Champneys was preparing to announce his preferred choice of Charles Knatchbull as major with Captains J A Wickham, T W Ledyard and S Dainton [6] when he was informed by William Sheppard to his 'utter astonishment and dismay' that Poulett had accepted Sheppard and his nominees for the situations. Champneys saw this as a plot by Sheppard and his cronies to take command and force him to resign, which he refused to do. On 13 November 1803 it was ordered by Lt General Tarleton, member of Parliament and military advisor, that all activities of the volunteer companies should be suspended until further orders.[7] In early December the Under-Secretary of State for the Home Department Reginald Pole-Carew also ordered that another attempt be made at reconciliation and that the matter of precedence should be decided by drawing lots or the companies be suspended. Again, Champneys refused claiming that it is 'utterly impossible for me to propose such a measure as a drawing of lots to ascertain a point already established'. He also claimed to be personally rather indifferent as to which company had precedence but his rank and file volunteers would not be moved.

The dispute became so bad that the matter was debated in Parliament with General Tarleton reporting that,

> ...a corps called the Selwood Forest Legion had actually refused to obey the orders of the General of Division, or the Lord Lieutenant, or any orders but those of their own officers. He had lamented this state of insubordination, and implored them to attend to their duty, but all in vain. Afterwards they showed so mutinous a spirit that they said they would rather fight it out on the parade than yield precedency to any other corps or submit to the orders of the Lord Lieutenant or General of Division and then actually formed themselves into an independent corp. He made a report of this alarming procedure to the War Office.

Sheppard and his followers agreed to follow orders and adopt the proposal that the matter should be decided by the drawing of lots and Poulett suggested to General Tarleton behind Champneys' back that his refusal to draw lots meant that he should be relieved of his command. They agreed further that the Frome companies should be split from Beckington and that the armaments stored at Orchardleigh should be delivered to them.

On Monday 12 March 1804 Thomas resigned – as did every man in the Beckington Company. He called them together and gave a long speech with selected readings from an archive of over 100 letters which had passed between him and the various parties involved. The resignation en masse of the men was perhaps an early indication of the respect he drew from the local populace and a precursor of what was to come almost 30 years later. Champneys produced a 60-page book outlining the dispute in the form of a *Letter to the Right Honourable The Earl Poulett* expressing his outrage at the reinstatement of his enemies.

Poulet had shown very weak leadership in the matter, changing his mind and sitting on the fence, and Champneys had not done himself many favours. The tone of much of his correspondence was alternately fawning, describing himself as a very humble individual, or puffed up and arrogant, often referring to his situation in life as a member of the aristocracy whose family had been in the area for seven centuries and how undeserving he was of such shoddy treatment.

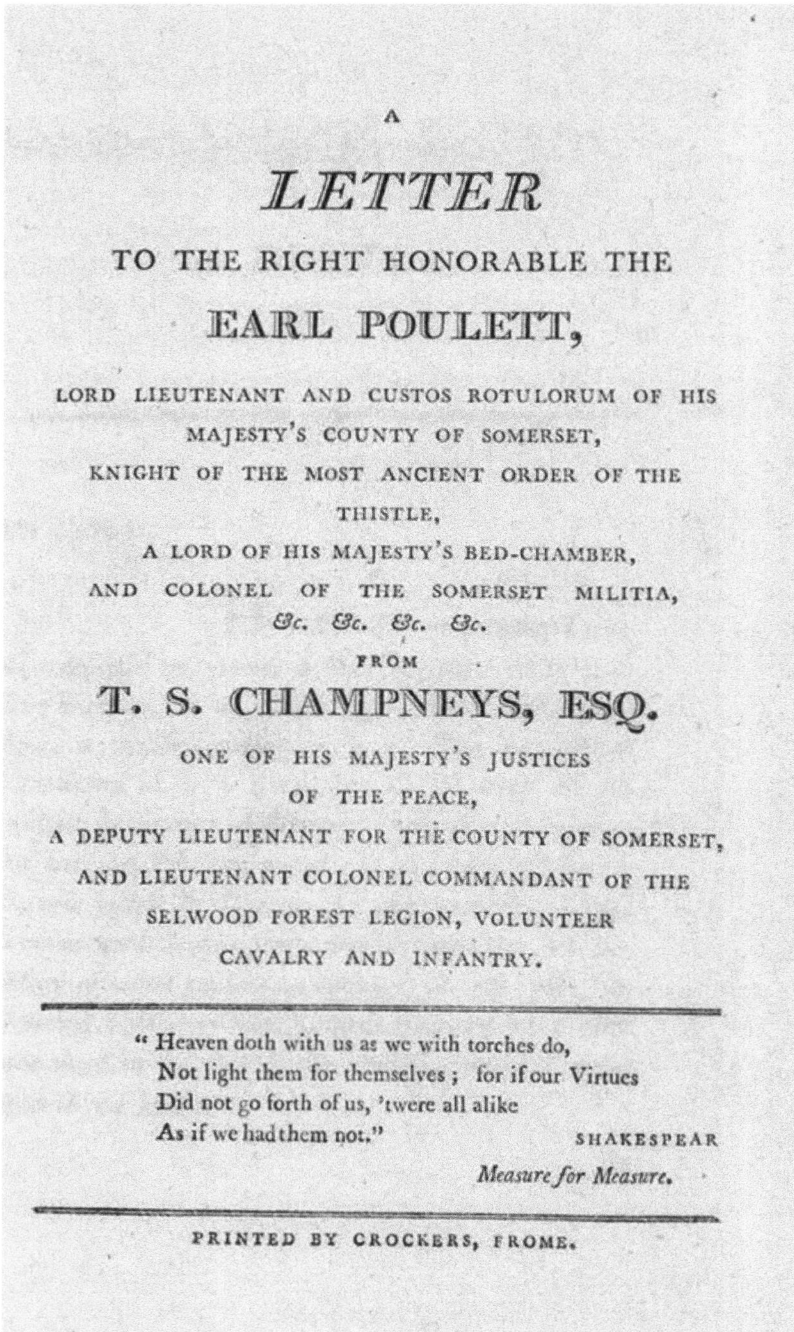

A

LETTER

TO THE RIGHT HONORABLE THE

EARL POULETT,

LORD LIEUTENANT AND CUSTOS ROTULORUM OF HIS MAJESTY'S COUNTY OF SOMERSET,
KNIGHT OF THE MOST ANCIENT ORDER OF THE THISTLE,
A LORD OF HIS MAJESTY'S BED-CHAMBER,
AND COLONEL OF THE SOMERSET MILITIA,
&c. &c. &c. &c.

FROM

T. S. CHAMPNEYS, ESQ.

ONE OF HIS MAJESTY'S JUSTICES OF THE PEACE,
A DEPUTY LIEUTENANT FOR THE COUNTY OF SOMERSET,
AND LIEUTENANT COLONEL COMMANDANT OF THE SELWOOD FOREST LEGION, VOLUNTEER CAVALRY AND INFANTRY.

"Heaven doth with us as we with torches do,
Not light them for themselves; for if our Virtues
Did not go forth of us, 'twere all alike
As if we had them not." SHAKESPEAR

Measure for Measure.

PRINTED BY CROCKERS, FROME.

William Sheppard was to die within a few months at his home in Styles Hill in Frome at the age of 42. At least some of the volunteers continued under the name of the Frome Selwood Volunteer Infantry and in September 1805 it was led by John Olive as major commandant and included the remaining Sheppards and James Slade.

BY WAY OF a postscript to all this, one of the groups of volunteers known as the 'Frome and East Mendip Volunteer Cavalry and Infantry', a command of some 400 men, was under the control of a Richard Badham Thornhill, Adjutant and Captain by brevet, (meaning an honorary rank awarded for merit). His name does not appear in any argument in relation to the previous matter but some months after the dispute, on 29 November 1804, he was found on the Orchardleigh estate with the Reverend Benjamin Richardson, rector of adjoining land at Farleigh Hungerford who, it seems, was often on the estate illegally, poaching game. The pair were apprehended by the gamekeeper, William Corner, who let fly with, 'Damn you! You are a damned rascally Adjutant and I'll get Mr. Champneys to write to the Duke of York to have you dismissed'!

Thornhill then verbally abused Corner in return and put his fowling piece to his shoulder within 12 inches of Corner's breast and threatened to shoot him. The immediate situation was resolved by the arrival of Champneys' gamekeeper Anthony Parker and the two trespassers withdrew. Champneys wrote to the officer commanding the volunteers Thomas Strangeways Horner of Mells Park complaining about Thornhill's conduct, which so incensed Thornhill that he wrote a very abusive reply to Champneys, part of which challenged him to a duel. Presumably infuriated by this and not one to pass up the opportunity of a day in court Champneys pressed charges against Richardson and Thornhill and the case was heard at the Bridgwater Assizes before Mr Baron Graham on 25 August 1805.

Richardson was tried first with Champneys demanding £100 in damages. He won his case as he often did but the jury awarded only one farthing in damages with one farthing in costs. The same charge was brought against Thornhill but the judge was tiring of such trivial matters and awarded a nominal verdict against him. The abusive letter, however, was another matter altogether; Thornhill was found guilty and remanded for sentencing to the King's Bench on 25 November. Realising the seriousness of his situation Thornhill had written to some influential friends of Champneys asking them to intercede on his behalf, expressing his contrition and sorrow at having written the letter and 'offering to make every atonement in his power by apologising in the fullest manner'. The fact that the apology was not offered until a few days before sentencing did not help his case. Champneys was unmoved and the sentencing went ahead.

Despite letters from James Wickham and others of the same regiment, supporting Thornhill's character, Mr Justice Grose, in pronouncing sentence, observed that the defendant was guilty of a very high offence, having sent a challenge to a gentleman to provoke him to commit a breach of the peace and to fight a duel. The letter was not only a challenge but contained a very gross libel which admitted of no extenuation whatever. For the protection of Mr Champneys and the public peace he was ordered to pay a fine of £50 and to be imprisoned in Marshalsea prison for three calendar months as well as entering into a security of £300 of his own money along with two further sureties of £150 to keep the peace for three years. It was further ordered that Thornhill remain in gaol until the fine was paid and the sureties found.[8]

Only a couple of years later in September of 1808 Robert Houlton, a naval lieutenant whose address was given as Farleigh Hungerford Castle, was also brought before the King's Bench for trespass on the Orchardleigh estate. Some years before in almost a carbon copy of the Thornhill case, Houlton was found in a wood by Sanders the gamekeeper who said he was surprised to see him there as he had been warned off before. In fact Houlton had been caught trespassing frequently and sometime before Champneys had written him what was described as 'a very civil letter' asking him to desist. Houlton's father saw the letter and told his son to stay away from the estate. Houlton responded with a furious letter to Champneys which he ended by saying that he was 'at any time, at his service' and these words were construed as a challenge to a fight. Champneys attempted to take him to court over this but the jury found that there was insufficient evidence and the case did not proceed.

After his father died in December 1805 Houlton began trespassing once more and was again discovered by the gamekeeper and during interrogation Champneys appeared accompanied by fellow magistrate, Mr Sainsbury. At this point Houlton walked up to Champneys, and nudged him with his elbow saying '.... you scoundrel, I am glad to meet you I have been a long while at Bath wishing to see you to give you the greeting which you deserve.' He also called him a brute, a scoundrel, a liar a grovelling toad and an owl, and said that, 'your name stinks in the country', and used all means to provoke and insult him, repeating 'that's a lie' at everything Champneys said. Champneys endeavoured to pacify him and remarked that he must be insane; he had been at some point acquainted with his brother John but did not know Robert Houlton at all.

Whilst Houlton was arguing, he held his double-barrelled shot gun on his arm horizontally towards Champneys and within two feet of his breast, the lock of each barrel was cocked. Eventually he was persuaded to lower the gun and go away. The outraged Champneys was far from satisfied and brought charges against him at the sessions, swearing that he believed if he had been alone the defendant's violence was so great that he would have killed him. He also believed that the defendant came upon him on purpose. Houlton made no defence other than to say that he was in the navy and had been absent from the neighbourhood for some years and was not aware that the ground he was shooting on belonged to his accuser. This was totally untrue and the origins of the whole matter lie several years before. It seems that the inhabitants of the parsonage house at Farleigh Hungerford had been in the habit of trespassing on the Orchardleigh estate for many years – since at least 1804 as we know from the Thornhill case.

Robert Houlton made no apology at his trial, which Champneys said he would have accepted and, despite a supporting reference from James Anthony Wickham, the court sentenced him to be imprisoned for six months in the King's Bench and to give two sureties of £250 each and himself of £500 – to be imprisoned until the sums were met.

It emerged that the Rector of Farleigh, Benjamin Richardson, was a good friend of the Houltons' as well as Thornhill and as we have seen he had been caught shooting partridge on the estate many times and had been warned off. Champneys was by now seriously annoyed by the errant vicar's constant trespassing and evolved a cunning plan to put a stop to it once and for all. Richardson lived in Woolverton because his official residence, the parsonage house, was rented to the Houlton family and this was in breach of an Act of Parliament which stipulated that a rector must not be absent from his parish for more than three months at a time. Richardson refused to give up what he claimed were his shooting rights, Champneys threatened to take him to court under this act of residency unless he did so, and in the August of 1807 that is exactly what he did. Richardson lost his case and Champneys was awarded £36 16s. 8d., being one third of the value of the living at Farleigh, plus costs. In an act of generosity, and despite his own debts, Champneys donated 20 guineas to the Governors of the Bath Hospital which was two-thirds of the total amount awarded to him.

~~~

In the midst of all the troubles with disobedient soldiers, poaching clergy and courtroom appearances, Mr and Mrs Champneys still found time for some light entertainment and were invited once more to a masquerade ball given by the Thellussons' at their London residence, Foley House, in early June 1804. The centrepiece was to have been a play and mock representation of Bonaparte's coronation, and scenery was acquired from Drury Lane with the various members of the gentry having learned their parts. This diversion was much discussed and reached the ears of an unnamed nobleman whose son was in France and who feared for his son's safety should it go ahead. The Thellusons were determined to continue with the performance, threatening to get a professional actor should their guests pull out. However, pressure was applied by an 'illustrious personage', possibly the Prince of Wales himself, and out of deference to him the play was abandoned in favour of a group of grotesque figures intended to personify the members of the, 'Society for the Suppression of Vice'.

The Prince Regent was once more in attendance, this time in the guise of a Highlander with his plaid cloak thrown over his shoulder, a hat looped up with a brilliant diamond button and a lofty white ostrich feather. Mrs Fitzherbert attended as a highland lassie. The garden was festooned with lamps and flowers as well as representations of the
~~~

Prince of Wales feathers. On the stage appeared a party of gods and goddesses with Apollo and the nine muses, which included the Duchess of Leeds and Mrs Champneys who sang. Thomas Champneys appeared in the guise of 'an old maid'.

A London journal covered the event in some detail and said that, 'any applause which the company might have bestowed, would be one of those sacrifices which judgement and truth too often make to politeness... [and he] did not think it consonant with the dignity and manliness of the English character. It had too much of those boulevard exhibitions in Paris which have so often, delighted Mr Thellusson'. It seems unlikely that this reporter was invited to future events.

Later that same month was the Duchess of Marlborough's Public Breakfast at Sion Hill. Attended by the Prince of Wales and Prince William of Gloucester along with 300 well-connected people, the equipage of Mr Champneys was judged to be 'amongst the most dashing'.

The *Morning Post* of 13 June 1804 reported on the Marchioness of Hertford's Rout[9] at Hertford House, Manchester Square, London attended by 700 people including Prince William of Gloucester. The Marchioness was later to become one of the mistresses of the Prince of Wales. Mr and Mrs Champneys were in attendance as was a Mr Beckford but no further details were published.

At the beginning of 1805 another Grand Ball was announced to take part at Orchardleigh to which all the fashionables for miles around were invited but no further details survive. On 17 May the fashionable couple were back in London for Mrs Dupre's Masquerade at Grafton Street. This was attended by the Prince of Wales and in excess of 1,000 people, and it can be claimed that Champneys truly excelled himself. He went dressed as a newspaper, the *Morning Post,* and gave some entertaining dissertations on the liberty of the press. This was the paper that followed the social lives of the rich and successful and often pointed out Champney's wit and good humour in its 'Fashionable World' column.

Just a couple of weeks later using the king's birthday as an excuse once more, Lady Lambert held a masquerade, in Little Argyle Street. Among the most prominent characters were two Roman Caesars, who

> supported their characters with such a fund of classic knowledge and

wit as has seldom been exhibited on similar occasions. The Duchess of Devonshire alone could combat their attacks. These characters were not recognised until the masks were withdrawn at supper when they were discovered to be those well-known votaries of wit and pleasantry William Spencer and Thomas Champneys. After supper Mr Spencer appeared as a Nestor Rosicus dressed as Young Norval attended by Mr Champneys as a modern dancing master teaching him to tread the stage with dignity and grace.

[1] Champneys, T. *A Letter to The Right Honourable the Earl Poulett, Lord Lieutenant and Custos Rotulorum of his Majesty's County of Somerset etc* 1804 SRO
[2] Frome Yearbook 17 p74 Richard Dellar
[3] *Gentleman's Magazine* 1840 p 205
[4] Batten Pooll p 175
[5] Gill Longleat papers Frome Museum D 1117
[6] Poulett letter p 19
[7] Poulett letter p 25
[8] Authentic Copies of Affidavits produced at the King's Bench Nov. 25 1805
[9] In Georgian England a "rout" was a relatively informal party given by the well-off, to which large numbers of people were invited. The term covered a variety of styles of event, but they tended to be basic, and a guest could not count on any music, food, drink, cards, and dancing being available, though any of these might be.

5
CHAMPNEYS v IRELAND
1806-1809

CHAMPNEYS' NEXT PUBLIC spat arose in October 1806 over the appointment of the sexton to St John's Parish Church in Frome. A sexton was an official with various practical duties including being in charge of the graveyard and fabric of the building. The previous holder of the position, John Deacon, had died and the vicar, William Ireland, (1754-1813) incumbent since 1793 and in a position that was the right of Lord Bath to fulfil, took it upon himself to appoint Deacon's son Robert in his place. Originally from Horningsham in Wiltshire, Ireland had

St John's Church Frome in the 1860s

studied for his MA at St John's College, Oxford and had married Alicia Everett at Horningsham in 1792. The Champneys family had, as lords of the manor, the right to appoint the sexton and had exercised this right for generations, promising the position on this occasion to a Richard Champneys Soane, so it came as some surprise when Robert Deacon turned up at Orchardleigh with a note,

> The vicar and principal inhabitants in Frome have desired me to call and request Squire Champneys will have the goodness to appoint me sexton to the church of Frome to succeed my father.

It is easy to imagine poor Robert nervously shuffling from one foot to the other knowing what the response was going to be and half expecting to have the dogs let loose upon him. The request was dismissed out of hand and a note sent back to Reverend Ireland,

> Orchardleigh October 21st 1806
> Sir,
> I beg to inform you that I have this day nominated Richard Soane to the office of sexton to the parish church of Frome, vacant by the death of John Deacon, and as it is my wish the person holding that situation should not be unacceptable to the resident clergyman, so am I to hope the present appointment will not be considered otherwise by you, and any injunction as to his duty that may be requisite in your judgement for the becoming conduct of the sexton, I shall feel it my duty, no less than a pleasure to attach to the appointment and,
> I am sir your obedient most humble servant,
> Thomas S Champneys.

Ireland's response the following day was equally to the point, and he was not going to concede without a fight,

> October 22nd 1806
> Sir,
> I am this morning favoured with your letter the contents of which I have communicated to the church wardens, who propose calling a vestry on the subject of it, the result of which you will be duly appraised of. I am

> very much obliged to you for your declaration of wishing to appoint a person acceptable to me, but what surely can I, or my parish, have of the proper conduct of a servant, who is not of our own appointment?
>
> I am sir your obedient most humble servant
>
> W. Ireland

The pair exchanged more terse notes in similar vein until Ireland sent the following,

> Notice is hereby given that a vestry will be held on Saturday at 11 o'clock in the morning – to consider of the claim made by Mr Champneys of a right to appoint a sexton to this church.

The notice was accompanied by a note inviting Champneys to bring documents supporting his claim along to the meeting – a suggestion which did not go down at all well and was designed to provoke. Outraged at the very suggestion that the word of a man in his position should be doubted and that he should have to prove anything, Champneys asked how Ireland would feel if asked to produce supporting evidence of his ordination or indeed documents to show that Lord Bath had the right to appoint him in the first place! The vestry meeting went ahead and as nothing had arrived in support of Champneys' claim they adjourned in order to inspect their own records, despite, according to Champneys,

> ...a full entry of vestry proceedings on the same subject in the year 1744... (which)... admit in the fullest manner.... the right of the Champneys family to the appointment in question, yet these wise-acres of the present day choose to reject this precedent.

Champneys made the very valid point that both the previous sexton and the one before that had been appointed by his family, in fact he was able to cite appointments going back generations. He claimed that Ireland had been to Orchardleigh and had already been shown the very documents that proved this right. This was a claim that Ireland vehemently denied, even offering to take an oath to that effect. Ireland persisted in his claim that the sexton was to be chosen by the church wardens and that he and his fellow clergymen should make the appointment, even suggesting in part conciliation and part insult that the duties could be split between the two men, one inside the church and one outside – with Champney's appointee confined to the churchyard of course. The vestry decided that Deacon's widow should carry out the duty of sexton until the matter could be resolved. Champneys appealed to his 'much honoured friend' Lord Bath for support and published his own letters to Bath, but not those in reply, 'not considering myself at liberty to publish his lordship's friendly communication to me on the subject' – Perhaps Bath was a little less supportive than had been hoped; Ireland was after all Bath's appointee.

As usual there was more to the matter than met the eye. Ireland's insistence on having Deacon's son appointed was fuelled by much personal dislike, there having been a dispute between the two sometime before, when Ireland claimed that part of a garden 'one mile deep in the parish of Orchardleigh'[1] was titheable to him, and also tried to claim tithes from some of the estate's tenants by issuing warrants of distress against them when sitting as a magistrate. The warrants left the tenants in total confusion as to whom they should pay their rent which resulted in one having his cows seized even though he had only been there for five months.[2]

The affair is referred to obliquely in Champneys' great poem *Hieromania* which is discussed in more detail below, one of the footnotes reads '...a vicar in the West of England once sat as a judge in his own cause to obtain tithes of certain lands in his neighbourhood, heretofore considered in another parish'...[3]

It was also the case that Ireland had little to lose by challenging his old enemy as he had persuaded the vestry to pay his legal fees out of the parish rates if he lost. Champneys accused Ireland of packing the vestry meeting with a small number of persons known to be discontented towards himself.[4] There was also the possibility of some objection to Soane personally. He was named as a charge on the estate of Richard Champneys to receive an annuity of £30 up to a total of £500[5] but exactly who he was is uncertain. He is described as having come 'from Fareham' in Hampshire where Richard had his estates and was born in around 1759 making him about ten years older than his sponsor, Thomas Swymmer. It is probable that he was the illegitimate son of Richard as the Champneys name obviously connects him to the family in some way and Richard's wife Jane had died in 1752. It is also likely that he was born shortly after the death of Richard as he is not mentioned in the will of 1759.

Soane or Sone as it was sometimes spelt, had been in partnership with a Joseph Cooke in Bath as 'mealmen' or grain dealers but the partnership ended in 1786 and Cooke continued on his own 'by mutual consent'. From 5 November 1800 Soane was an inmate of the King's Bench prison for debt until his release under a new insolvency act[6] on 1 March 1801 when he was discharged. His debts amounted to over £500 and a meeting of creditors took place during February 1802. How the debts arose is not known but he is described as a miller in one of the notices and presumably it was connected to his recent partnership with Cooke.

Whatever his pedigree, Soane turned up for work at St John's on 12 November 1806 but was denied entry by Ireland and his two church wardens John and William Baynton. In February of 1807 local solicitor and worthy Thomas Bunn was dispatched to Orchardleigh in the faint hope that Champneys would accept the compromise of appointing his nominee to the churchyard only – and was politely shown the door.

Neither side would give way and in the firm belief that all legal advice and documentary evidence supported his case Champneys took the matter to the Court of King's Bench, and the case of *Thos. S. Champneys Esq. v the Vicar of Frome and others,* was heard in Westminster on 10 June 1807.[7] The result was an outright victory for Champneys with the issue of a writ of mandamus recognising that,

> from time immemorial the family of Champneys has exercised the right of appointing a sexton at Frome with no interruption...except that in the year 1743 when one Thomas Baily who had been appointed sexton by Richard Champneys after enjoying the office for a few years and conducting himself extremely improper by habitual drunkenness mistaking one grave for another he received notice forbidding him to dig any grave or enter the church yards and (was) demanded the keys of the church which he refused to give up causing fresh locks and keys to be procured.[8]

Lionel Seaman, the vicar at that time, along with the churchwardens, had appointed their own man and were challenged in court by Richard Champneys, Thomas Swymmer's grandfather; Champneys won and Baily was briefly reinstated before Champneys chose a more upright successor.

Over 60 years later history was repeating itself and the earlier case was detailed in the vestry records to which Ireland refused access. The court was told that the case arose 'from a spirit of revenge and personal pique (and that) the present possessor (of the rights) was attacked and impeded in many of his ancient rights as Lord of the Manor of Orchardleigh and other estates and particularly in this instance...'

Ireland and his vestry ignored the order, they 'did not or would not obey the writ as they were commanded but on the contrary wholly neglected and refused to do so (and they), falsely fraudulently and deceitfully say that Richard Champneys Soan was not duly nominated'.[9]

The case was returned to court and on 26 August 1808 in front of Justice Bayley sitting at Wells who, after hearing much evidence of previous sexton's appointments, accepted Champneys' case and it was again ordered that Ireland admit Soane to the office of sexton forthwith. Still Ireland would not give up and to Champneys' astonishment managed to convert James Wickham, confidential attorney and steward to the family, as was his father before him, to bring forward 'evidence' that the Champneys family had no right to the manors of Orchardleigh or Frome Selwood! Ireland, in one final move, tried to get the judgement set aside and applied for a new trial. Lord Chief Justice Ellenborough had the final word, stating that he had, 'attentively read the notes of his brother Bayley, who tried the suit at Wells and did not consider there was the smallest pretence to ground an application for a new trial'.

On 4 December of that year Richard Champneys Soane was duly installed, the church wardens being ordered to deliver to him, 'the keys of the belfry and the greens (upon which he), took corporal possession of his said office by tolling the great bell'. How he got on with his new colleagues is not recorded but his reign was relatively short, as he died soon after and was buried in St John's churchyard on 23 November 1812 leaving his estate to his widow Elizabeth.[10] Ireland died the following year; and was also buried in the churchyard. His legal costs amounted to £135, which was paid by the parishioners of Frome. Champneys estimated his costs in the case to have been in the order of £800 and in a document in the Wiltshire Record Office quoted by Michael McGarvie he claimed his total costs in all litigation by 1815 to have exceeded £10,000.

~~~

DESPITE ALL THE legal shenanigans there was still time to party, and 4 June 1807 saw the annual celebration of the king's birthday again at St James Palace as he entered his 69th year; Mrs Champneys emerged in a, 'white crêpe body and train trimmed with a lace petticoat of the same and draperies fastened with large bunches of wallflowers'. The antics of her husband were not reported on this occasion but sometime later at the Marchioness of Buckingham's masquerade he became Counsellor Bother'em with a pocketful of briefs. This character, it was reported, was replete with talent and humour attracting universal notice.

The following year Wednesday 4 June 1808 was the occasion of the king's 70th birthday, with the celebrations taking place once more at St James Palace. The king did not attend in person due to failing eyesight but the queen and the Prince of Wales were there in person as was Mrs Champneys in a' train and body of primrose coloured crêpe trimmed with point lace petticoat of the same, at the bottom a border to correspond with the draperies which were appliqued in a style quite nouvelle, with dark brown leaves of tulips falling'. [11]Once more Thomas isn't mentioned by name amongst the long list of attendees but it is hard to imagine him having missed it.

In October of 1808 Prince William, Duke of Gloucester, one of the grandsons of King George II and someone who the Champneys might have known pretty well, as they often attended the same fashionable London parties, came to dine at Orchardleigh. Despite being out of the direct royal line he was a stickler for royal protocol and like his host the general estimate of his mental capacity was not great, as is illustrated by his nickname, 'Silly Billy'. He was visiting Bath at the time and according to the local papers 'condescended to dine with several of the principal residents'. He was apparently 'much gratified with the reception he met from his worthy hosts' at Orchardleigh. To celebrate the visit Thomas named the magnificent and elaborate gothic gateway to his estate Gloucester Lodge in the Duke's honour. The date of its construction is
~~~

not known but it was certainly completed by 1818, as a drawing of that date confirms.[12] Over the gateway to the lodge itself carved into the stone is the family arms with the date 1434, presumably an event in the family history, real or imagined now lost to us. John Skinner the antiquarian and vicar of Camerton described it in 1825, rather unkindly as '... the absurd castellated gateway the incarcerated Sir Thomas Champneys made as an entrance to his grounds'.[13] It still stands today facing on to Lullington Lane. Huge debt didn't seem to curb his enthusiasm for display and as part of the same attempt to impress he built a large banqueting hall and had the twin lodges at the Murtry entrance to the estate constructed in the 1820s.

Towards the end of September 1808 came the sad news that Peter Thellusson, by then Baron Rendlesham, had died while out shooting with Louis XVIII and the Earl of Chatham on his Suffolk estate at the age of 46. Foley House was purchased by Champneys' friend and fellow party-goer Prince William of Gloucester and demolished not long after.[14] The parties continued, at least for a while. In June 1809 Mrs Richards held a Grand Masquerade Ball at her home in Grosvenor Square. This was attended by the Marchioness of Bath and Mrs Champneys who appeared as Venetian ladies with 'both looking beautiful' according to the London papers. Mr Champneys appeared in an excellent mask supported with his usual good humour, calling himself Lady Belinda Blossom, and was admirably supported by his companion Viscountess Melbourne as Lady Teresa Tulip.

That same month was Mrs Boehm's Party at St James Square and 'Mr Champneys was there as a French dancing master of the old school and led off Lady Coventry's Minuet most admirably with Mrs Boehm. His appearance attracted as much notice as his constant succession of rich and good humour; he was extremely well dressed in a white satin coat, embroidered with roses etc. The ladies were all extremely anxious to take a lesson'.

Among Champneys' close friends was Edmund Boyle, the 8th Earl of Cork and Orrery, who had fought in the Revolutionary and Napoleonic wars, and his wife Lady Isabella. By October 1809 they had produced seven out of an eventual tally of nine children and a fete was organised in their honour beside the lake at Orchardleigh prompting Champneys to pen one of his poems,

THE LADY OF THE LAKE

Up rose the sun, his dancing beams
With every line were gay;
He shone on fields by Ceres loved,
But smiled on ORCHARDLEIGH.

He eyed De Merlaund's[1] ancient dome,
The forest old, the brake,
The upland lawn, the fertile glen,
The rippling lucid lake.

Blest be the power that form'd the scene,
For every purpose bland,
Where willing Taste to CHAMPNEYS lends
Her all directing wand!

Where Charlotte too, with eye benign,
From MOSTYN'S[2] honour'd race,
Gives to the whole the happy charm
That decks-adorns the place.

This day- she bade the playful oars
The glossy surface break;
This day she rained o'er liquid realms-
The Lady of the Lake!

Around her drew an infant group,
Of MARSTON'S[3] chieftains born
Oh! may they hence like other BOYLES,
Their country's page adorn!

The Virtues-Arts-begem'd the shore,
Attracted by the *Name*;
The Muse too shared the festive day,
And dwells upon the theme.

Pan-Satyrs-Fanns-the Dryads laugh'd
They gambol'd on the brink,
Well knowing that no adverse fate
The jocund[4] crew could sink.

Fair Plenty fill'd her fluted horn,
Display'd the bounteous treat,
And led the Lord of ORCHARDLEIGH
To take his cheerful seat.

He did – and bade his favour'd guests
Of every good partake;
In Welcome's throne delighted sat,
The Lady of the Lake .

She'd quitted now her shelly car,
To fill on shore her place,
Another Lady Bountiful,
The festive board to grace.

The Muses follow'd, sung anew
Sir Amyan[5]: Champneys' sire -
While ORCHARDLEIGH responsive rung
To Cambria's sweetest lyre.

Too soon came night – descending Sol
His race reluctant clos'd:
On Virtue's lap the rural group
With grateful hymn repos'd.

LLWYD

1 Sir Henry de Merland was a celebrated warrior and contemporary with Edward III to whose grandfather, Henry Orchardleigh had been transferred by Henry de la Culture, *temp.* Edward I. To this family succeeded that of Romesey, the heiress of which brought it to the Champneys, a family who came over with the Conqueror and who now

Gloucester Lodge Orchardleigh 1818 [15]

possess it.

2 Mrs. Champney's daughter of the late Sir Roger Mostyn, of Mostyn in the county of Flint, bart.

3 The seat of the Earl of Cork and Orrey

4 Alludes to the buoyancy of *Cork*

5 Sir Amyan Champneys.

The 25 October 1809 was the golden jubilee of King George and of course one more excuse for an extravagant party at Orchardleigh.

The union flag was displayed by break of day and after the family had attended the service at the church 50 poor persons were regaled with excellent meat etc; at seven in the evening a most magnificent bonfire, accompanied by a display of skyrockets and discharges of artillery illuminated the surrounding country. The whole spot being covered by joyous people in their Jubilee clothes. At 9 o'clock music summoned the different groups to the mansion when upwards of 50 persons consisting solely of the tenantry, their wives, sons and daughters sat down to a plentiful supper and after drinking his Majesty's health with three times three and imploring every blessing on him the merry pipe and harp were introduced and each loyal youth singled out his partner in the dance till day break summoned them to their different avocations. Nothing could exceed the regularity and decorum of the whole of this rustic fete.

Philanthropy was never far from Champney's mind and in 1812 he was one of the signatories of a letter to the Mayor of Bath requesting that he convene a meeting at the Guildhall to form a branch of the British and Foreign Bible Society. This was duly established and Thomas became one of the vice presidents, contributing 5gns and an annual subscription. The same year he was one of a number of local worthies who became founder members of The Bath and Wells Diocese Society for the Education of the Infant Poor in the Principles of the Established Church. He sat as vice president with a number of other noblemen, gentlemen and clergymen. He contributed a donation of £20 and promised an annual subscription of £2.2s. 0d.

[1] Champneys, T.S. *A Narrative of the proceedings with the particulars of the trial at Wells in the month of August 1808 relative to the appointment of a sexton to the parish church of Frome Selwood.* 1809. (Frome Public Library)
[2] Singer Frome Worthies 1893. Frome Yearbook 2004
[3] *Hieromania* p 22 footnote
[4] *Narrative* 1809 p 82
[5] *An Act* 1770
[6] *Act for the relief of certain insolvent debtors...* 1801
[7] *Narrative* 1809 p 57
[8] *Narrative* 1809 p 82
[9] *Narrative* 1809 p 46
[10] Ancestry
[11] Public Ledger 1806-06-05
[12] Richard Cox map of 1818 SRO
[13] Journals of John Skinner add ms.33681 British Library
[14] Wikipedia
[15] SRO

6
IRELAND v CHAMPNEYS 1811-1813

Soane's appointment as sexton to St John's was by no means the end of the affair. Thomas Champneys was not a man to forgive and forget – or to quit while he was ahead. In 1808 two pamphlets appeared, one entitled, *Minutes of the Proceedings in the Election of a Sexton,* and the other a poem entitled *Hieromania* or 'religious frenzy', these were published by John Macdonald, a bookseller and printer of 3 Harris's Place, Oxford Street in London. They were unsigned and circulated to clergy and gentry throughout the parish and county; Rev Ireland thought them to be grossly libellous as the first accused him of packing the vestry meeting to ensure the election of his candidate as well as attacking his character and accusing him of the dereliction of his duties as a magistrate and cleric. The poem went further as the author, 'not only attacked Mr Ireland himself but .... had the meanness the unmanliness and pusillanimity to attack Mrs Ireland and some of her friends in language the most vulgar, mean and scurrilous'.

Hieromania[1] is the only one of the two books known to have survived and consists of a 54-page 127 stanza poem, humorous, obscure and surreal in equal measure. It seems that only 22 copies were printed and the 'Preface by the Editor' is addressed to 'The Worthy and Respectable Inhabitants of F[rome]'[2] and purports to be the story of a man from Frome telling his story from the condemned cell. His situation arose from an 'early indulgence' in such venial crimes as robbing orchards, smuggling, unlawfully destroying game and poaching. His skills were always much in demand by local gangs, with whom he poached from Longleat, Mells and Orchardleigh amongst other estates. There follows the rather gnomic passage, 'When in that populous and factious town any legal right was to be disputed with the aristocracy of the neighbourhood he was generally the ringleader and he confessed with thorough contrition, that soon after the union with Ireland, it was he who stirred up and fomented the clamours against the appointment of a sexton to the parish church of Frome which the possessor of Orchardleigh justly claimed, and laid the foundation of that rancorous and disgraceful opposition'.

The 'author' also confesses to the 'plunder of a country bank' which 'caused him to submit to voluntary exile from his beloved town' and to lose himself in the 'long town' where, changing his name he got in with a gang of housebreakers and was at last to be executed for burglary with a strong suspicion of murder.

The unnamed author and felon owed an 'inveterate grudge' against the 'intrepid magistrate of O[rchardleigh]' who had often frustrated his villainy'. While in prison awaiting the hangman, he penned the poem *Hieromania* and passed it to his hoped-for editor along with a five-pound note to pay for its publication.

This bizarre tale of the work's origin seems to contain too much detail to be pure invention and must be based on some genuine individual. He was possibly a composite of several of Champneys enemies, but it has not as yet proved possible to decipher the names of them all. The poem was intended for a limited audience who would have recognised immediately the people named only by initials, some can be identified with reference to the signed documents reproduced in the *Narrative,* considered later, – a sort of very long in-joke.

In an obvious reference to Ireland's alleged visit to peruse various documents at Orchardleigh the poet writes,

Has't thou then O[rchardleigh] forgot,
It's wine, its fatted haunch
When at my table thou wert wont
To cram thy monstrous paunch[3]

The *Minutes* were distributed first, wrapped in brown paper, to Lord Cork, Tom Horner of Mells, The Marquis of Bath and various other local gentry as well as local magistrates and clergymen; a short time later the same gentlemen received copies of *Hieromania*. Incensed by these attacks on his reputation and that of his wife Ireland took the matter to court in February 1811. The printer, Macdonald at first denied that he had anything to do with *Hieromania* but an apprentice gave evidence to show that he had assisted his master in the production of the work. There was no way out for Mr Macdonald whose name and address was firmly attached to the *Minutes* as the publisher, printer and distributor; he admitted the libel but refused to name the author insisting that he did not know who it was. In mitigation Macdonald swore that he had printed only 30 copies, did not know, 'to whom the initials referred' (many of the people caricatured in the poem are referred to only by initials) and that he had made a trip to Frome 'to make atonement to the prosecutor'. The prosecution, in the form of the Attorney General, was not impressed and informed the court that although he could not contradict any of the mitigation it was probably worth drawing the court's attention to the fact that the prisoner was defended by Mr Garrow who was Mr Champneys attorney...

Libel against a man of the cloth, a magistrate and noted member of the community was not a matter to be taken lightly and poor Macdonald paid a heavy price for his evasive silence – six calendar months in Marshalsea prison, undoubtedly the foulest in the country, followed by entering into a recognisance of £100 for his good behaviour for three years.

Doubtless spurred on by his success and as unforgiving as his opponent, Ireland was keen to return to the fray and in the early part of 1813 he made a bid for the main prize and took Thomas Champneys himself to court. This time it was for yet another publication the, *Narrative of Proceedings with the Particulars of the Trial that took place at Wells in the month of August Relative to the Appointment of a Sexton to the Parish Church of Frome Selwood* ... This was produced a year after the other two in 1809, and on its flyleaf it stated quite clearly, 'Compiled and Arranged by Thomas Swymmer Champneys Esq'. This too had been published by the unfortunate John Macdonald; there could be no question of the account's authorship and it seems that Champneys did not contest the libel action and judgement was entered against him by default. Possibly this account was a repetition of the already proven libels in the *Minutes* and any defence would have been costly and pointless. In another turnaround Champneys' counsel admitted that he was 'connected' to the scurrilous poem *Hieromania*. The only point at issue was the amount of damages to be awarded, and an enquiry to determine this was held at the Somerset Assizes before a special jury at the beginning of April. In Champneys' favour was an agreement by most who had read the publications that, 'they continued to have the same opinion of Mr Ireland after reading the libels as they had before and Mr Ireland's character was too well established to be hurt by any anonymous letter writer'. Despite this Mr Serjeant Pell for Ireland demanded the enormous sum of £3,000 in compensation. The jury consulted for a few moments before agreeing that damages should be set at £1,500.

It was now that Champneys received a very welcome stroke of good fortune – Ireland died on 8 April 1813 at the age of 59 and as he died before the order could be formally entered, the judgement for damages was set aside. His relief was short lived. Alicia Ireland, the vicar's widow, decided to sue on her own account and the case was revived. In September she put forward a claim for £5,000 on the grounds that parts of the poem referred directly to her and were of a 'cruel and libellous tendency'. Thomas West was sent to serve the writ at Orchardleigh and seems to have been rather brusque when meeting Champneys, resulting in an altercation between the two and Champneys being taken to court for assault and false imprisonment. This time he lost and West was awarded £150 damages.[4] Champneys thought the incident important enough to produce yet another of his pamphlets.[5] Interestingly Mr West was one of the signatories on the *Narrative of the Frome Riot* that we shall come to in a later chapter.

When it came to court Mr Lens for Champneys contended that the passages produced in evidence were so weak and trivial that they could command only nominal damages. The printer John Macdonald appeared as a witness and having taken his pledge to be of good behaviour to heart, gave evidence that he was employed to produce the pamphlets and paid by Thomas Champneys.

Details of the extracts examined by the court have not survived but the poem itself has, and the more comprehensible parts at the end of the work relating to Alicia include,

> As from her orial window look'd
> The priest's virago wife,

And found a damp had paralys'd
The abettors of the strife.
*
Found that her deary never stirr'd
His voluble red rag
That W[illiam] C[hislett] Kingdom come[6]
and all began to flag
*
Enraged she to the kitchen went.
And in her furious hand,
Plac'd on the fire, to roast the beef,
She seized a flaming brand
*
Cries she! "you dastard Blueskin herd
Why stare ye like stuck pigs!
And have you suffered Orchardleigh
On you to run his rigs.
*
And does my bullying husband too
Desert his favourite plan?
Borrow my amazonian nerve
Thou chicken-hearted man
*
With that she tossed her brand on high'
All eager to destroy,
And as she vengeful rushed along
The furies shrieked for joy
*
So shoots a comet through the sky'
In the same wild attire,
Restricted to no certain course,
Its tail a stream of fire.
*
But as to execute her threat
The churchyard path she sought
Alas! the sacrilegious flame
Her floating muslin caught

*

Straight "Kingdom come" this saw, and thought
Of Baptist Chapel Pool,
And there the blazing heroine drove
In hopes her fire to cool

*

The more she hurried through the air
More furiously she burn'd
And e'er she could be fairly dipp'd
Was to a cinder turned.

*

The V[icar] followed like a shot
To see what was become,
Of wife and preacher, and to quench
Her conflagrated B(u)m

*

He came to smell a sulph'rous stench
And see his wife a coal,
But came, alas! too late to save
Her body or her soul.

*

Then to the consecrated flood
He, in despair, plunged in,
And instantly to the bottom went,
So heavy was his sin.

The tale continues with the bodies being dragged from the pond and refused burial in the church

The pious men of F[rome] were heard
Like doctrine to maintain,
And vow'd if in the church yard laid,
To dig him up again

The pair are adjudged suicides and buried at the crossroads,

At Blacksbridge, name of horrid sound,

For horrid deeds designed,
Where roads to intersect are seen,
Appropriate place they find.

There is a footnote by the name 'Blacksbridge',[7]

In thus fixing on Blacksbridge the author has shewn his thorough knowledge of the life and character of his hero, who for some considerable time had an intrigue on his hands with a labourer or gardener's daughter in the immediate neighbourhood. Not an inconvenient circumstance when returning from the sumptuous board of his excellent patron. Hot with the Tuscan grape and high in blood. Vide. Fair Penitent.

The surreal and humorous lines regarding Alicia could be excused as a bit of fun but to accuse her husband of having an affair must surely be libellous, unless of course, it was true. Blacksbridge lies between Frome and Lord Bath's seat at Longleat. The poem ends after 127 stanzas with Ireland and his wife haunting the crossroads where they are buried and assuming hideous ghostly forms at night. The jury were out for over eight hours before bringing in a verdict in Mrs Ireland's favour with damages set at £400 a far cry from the £5,000 she had hoped for.

There can be no doubt that Champneys is the sole author of the pamphlets, signed and unsigned – who else would bother? He takes great delight in quoting part of the poem and seems infatuated with his own cleverness as he describes it; -

The witty, and, learned author of a lively poem entitled *The Hieromania* which made its appearance in this country, from an anonymous pen immediately after the trial at Wells and which certainly is no less replete with naked truths, than poetic fiction says,

"Mandamus" that's an ugly word!
What means it? parson say!
Perhaps it means for all your jokes
The piper we must pay.

And very truly has this merry rogue depicted the feelings of most of the early opponents to this appointment being vested in my family...'[8]

~~~

When he wasn't sorting out his own troubles he was sitting as a magistrate and sorting out those of others. A remarkable survival from these years are the journals of Isaac Gregory who was Constable of Frome from 1813-14 and again during 1817-18. Gregory describes Champneys as 'by far the best magistrate'.[9] In January of 1814 Gregory was called out to a sordid and unusual case. In his journal for 18 January he records that 'A married woman came with her husband to get redress against a married man for an assault and ill treatment of her person'. She gave evidence as follows.

> I was at Mr Bayleys at the Weymouth Arms[10] having a pint of beer when I had occasion to go the privy your honour. This man came after me and said he would come in... he pushed me about and used me very ill your honour and I left the place without doing what I went to do. After a while I went to the privy a second time to do what I could not do the first time and he followed again your honour, Now your honour could I not sware a rape against this man?
>
> Champneys asked the man for his version and was told, Sir she compelled me to do it. As my witnesses will prove she went out on purpose for me to follow her. And when we came back here is a witness that asked her whether he had done it and she said he had, and should again, and then we had a quart each together.
>
> The magistrate was having none of it and gave the husband a stern lecture on not looking after his wife and letting her go to Public Houses drinking. The woman was disbelieved because she did not cry out and, should have resisted his coming in and with the noise which he must have made forcing an entry added to the shrieks which you ought to have made would have made people in the house hear you.

The accused was given a severe reprimand for carrying on in this fashion as a married man and the case was dismissed. The woman's husband was then worried about his position and asked Champneys to get his wife to swear that the man did not violate her person in the privy,
~~~

because if she did not swear it he would think that she 'did it' and he should not live happily with her. Eventually the woman swore on oath that the man tried to do it but did not and Champneys told the husband that he may now 'put up your two fingers and smooth down your hair, and that he should now live happy for he could believe his wife to be a virtuous woman'. Gregory's final comments were 'Ah, you poor fool, thou art a fool of the lowest order'.[11]

Champneys financial problems continued and in 1814 he agreed to convey the reversionary interest in the Orchardleigh estate to Richard Henry Cox, his mother Caroline Cox's brother, an army agent and banker, in return for Cox paying of some of his debts to an amount not exceeding £65,000, – when he died Cox would have possession of the estate. [12]

[1] Please see Appendix for a fascinating discussion of one aspect of this poem.
[2] Where initials have been substituted for complete words for names or places brackets have been used between the missing letters.
[3] Stanza 21
[4] Pooll p176
[5] Champneys, TS *Facts attending the prosecution of Thomas Swymmer Champneys one of the magistrates of the County of Somerset for an alleged assault and false imprisonment preferred by Thomas West.* Bristol pub Joseph Routh, Narrow Wine St. 1815 Not seen
[6] The initials fit William Chislett one of the signatories of the various vestry proclamations and Ireland's lawyer at the trial. 'Kingdom come' is probably reference to another, George Kingdon.
[7] Today the area known as Blatchbridge
[8] Narrative 1809 p 37
[9] McGarvie *Crime and Punishment* p12
[10] Now the Old Bath Arms in Palmer St.
[11] McGarvie *Crime and Punishment* p15
[12] SRO DD\DU 3-5-7

7
1814 THE DOG, THE BAILIFF AND THE JUDGE

FOR MANY YEARS Champneys had caused what were described as 'cautionary boards' to be placed around his Orchardleigh estate informing all and sundry that any dogs found upon his land were to be destroyed. In February of 1813 Ralph Crosier, one of his most trusted servants, variously described as the estate's game-keeper, butler and housekeeper, engaged an assistant with the wonderful name of Zachariah Broderib whom he had instructed to rid the woods and plantations on the estate of all dogs and vermin. Champneys claimed that he had had 50 head of 'beautiful deer' destroyed during five successive Saturday nights by two dogs which were only destroyed by having ten armed men to hunt them down and destroy them, and he was determined to stop any re-occurrence of the situation. Broderib complained to his boss about a greyhound bitch, the property of William Corner who leased an estate of 51 acres at Laverton bordered by Cock Road and the Orchardleigh Estate. Not content that his own lands 'abounded with game' it seems that Corner was constantly hunting young hares and rabbits on Champneys property. Corner has of course appeared before as he was Champneys' gamekeeper at the time of the Thornhill affair of 1805, but they had fallen out and he doubtless bore a grudge or two.

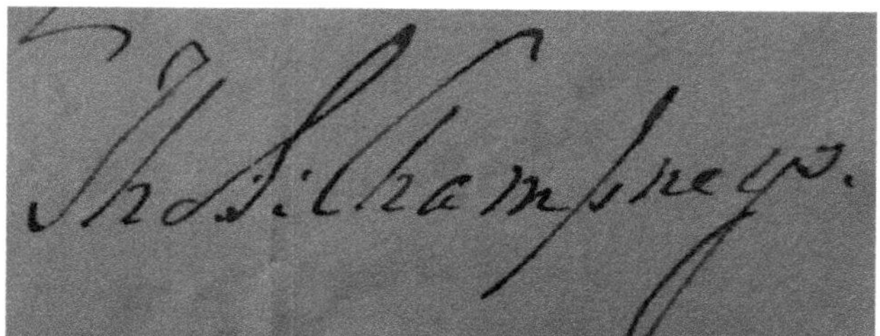

Signature of Thomas Swymmer Champneys

The dog was caught and destroyed which resulted in Champneys and Crozier being taken to the Taunton Assizes of March 1814 by Corner who was claiming damages for his loss. There are two distinct accounts of the course of events. According to Corner, the plaintiff, Crosier went to his house in Cock Road, took the dog to Orchardleigh, tied her to the stump of a tree and ordered Broderib to shoot her before burying the body. To bolster his claim Corner brought forward 'several sporting gentlemen' who according to Champneys, were simply friends of Corner, to say that if the dog had been theirs they would not have taken 50 or even 100 guineas for her.[1]

The defence case was that the dog was a seven-year-old poaching dog which had been found in the grounds of Orchardleigh and destroyed in accordance with the warning signs posted around the estate. Broderib's evidence for the plaintiff was untrue and vindictive, they claimed, as he had been dismissed by Champneys in May 1813 for gross misconduct and was seeking revenge. Not only that but both he and Corner had been sentenced under the game laws previously by Champneys in his role as magistrate resulting in Broderib being sent to prison. Champneys stated that his orders were that any dogs found hunting alone on the estate would be destroyed, his own included, and if this order was not obeyed the servant responsible would be dismissed. His Honour was having none of it and ordered the jury to return a verdict in Corner's favour and set the damages at £50 stating that Champney's actions were simply wrong in law and that 'no gentleman, no matter how exalted his station had the right to destroy dogs of any description whether trespassing or not'.[2] A very disappointing result.

During the same period and despite all his financial troubles in August 1814 Champneys was said to be about to erect a column 100 feet high to celebrate the peace with France and the restoration of the Bourbons, with a medallion of his friend the Prince Regent at its base. Sadly for future generations but fortunately for his finances this never came about.

Within months of his defeat over the dog, Champneys had more trials to contend with. The ill-advised poem *Hieromania* refused to go away and on 13 August 1814, at the Somerset Assizes in Wells six years after its publication, Champneys was taken to court once more. Doubtless buoyed up by Alicia Ireland's belated award of £400 the

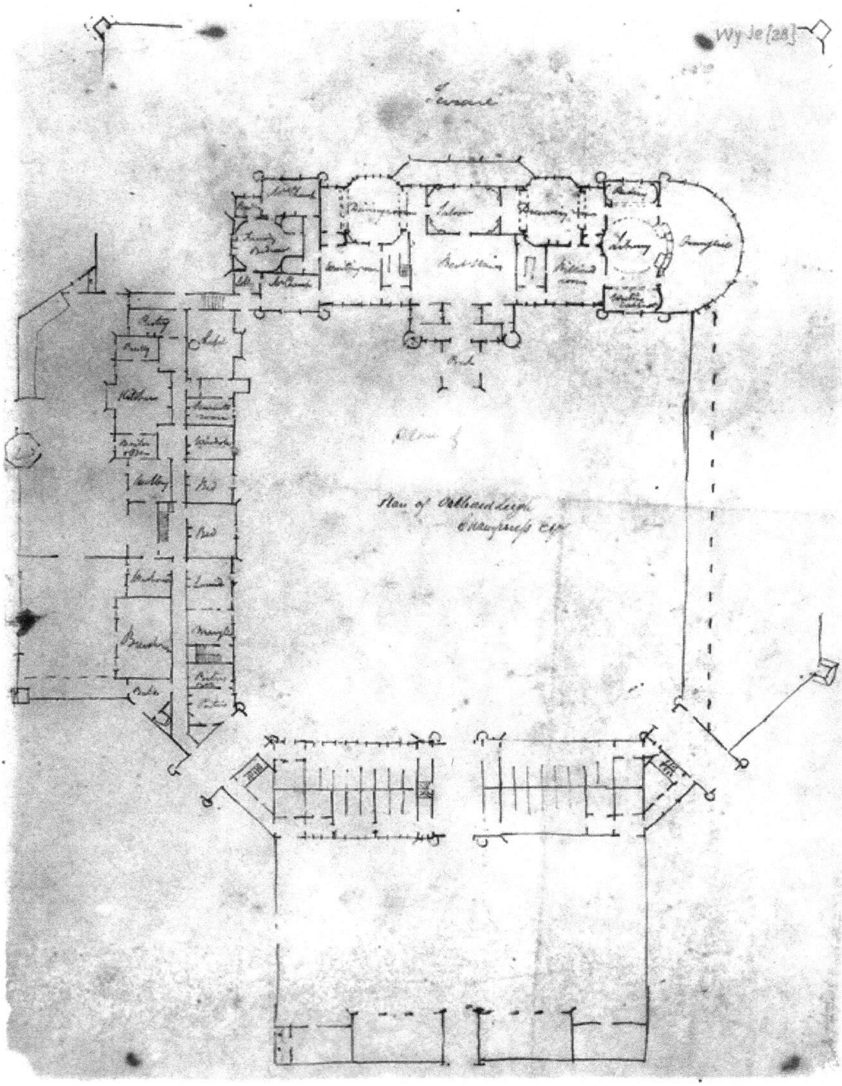

A plan of the old house at Orchardleigh (M.McGarvie)

previous September, George Kingdon a local clothier decided to try his luck claiming £1000 for damage to his reputation, despite Serjeant Lens for Champneys describing him as 'a fanatic, a democrat, and a mischief working character'. The defence position was that no damage had been done or could be proved, the publication was years old and the prosecution was malicious and vindictive. The jury, to the astonishment of the court and Judge Dampier, awarded Kingdon £100 in damages. A statute of limitations meant that the time for bringing such an action was very close to its end and this had presumably been a factor in bringing the case at this time.

At the beginning of September 1814, it was announced in the *Bath Chronicle* that a book was to be published entitled *The Trial of John McDonald, Printer* which was to contain detailed accounts of all four trials for libel that the poem had generated. This was to include the full text of *Hieromania* and was to be published by a Messrs. Clarke and Co priced at 3/- The advertisement continues,

> As the reports of the above trials all relate to the same book and as it appears that only 22 copies of this poem were ever printed and the different reports of the four trials include the whole of the poem, preface and notes, it may not prove uninteresting to such persons as have not read the book that has become of so much notoriety.

However, another notice in the same newspaper for the 27 October reported,

> HIEROMANIA!!! A POEM
> Messrs. Clarke and Co. beg leave to inform the public that the REPORT of the four different TRIALS upon the subject of this poem is unavoidably delayed publication in consequence of certain letters they have received upon the subject....
>
> Those orders they have received for the book will be punctually attended to.

Unfortunately, if the book was ever printed or distributed there is now no trace of it and it is probable that the threat of more actions for libel caused the publishers to cancel it.

~~~

IN AUGUST 1815 Champneys was again arrested along with Ralph Crozier, his housekeeper, Thomas Atkinson, his postillion, and John
~~~

West a former stable boy now employed in the house. On 28 October 1814 John White, a butcher and occasional bailiff from Bath, attended Orchardleigh along with an assistant named Baker, with two warrants to seize goods to the value of about £350. White's evidence was that upon arrival at 6.00pm he and Baker were violently assaulted, their warrants taken from them and thrown into the fire by Champneys and consumed. White claims that he was then dragged violently through the passage by the order and with the assistance of Champneys for the purpose of being thrown into a pond, by which action they nearly choked him. He begged for his life and said that if they would let him go he would give up the process. To this appeal Mr Champneys answered, 'Will he? Then chain him up in the stable to the manger'. White claims that in the struggles he was violently assaulted, wounded and bled profusely from the nose.

The defence case was that it was the bailiffs who had committed the assaults. Champneys defended himself in person and in a speech of considerable length complained that he was the injured party and had been marked out for ruin by Edmund Broderip and Co. for the past 12 years. They were the undersheriffs through whose hands many thousands of pounds worth of his property had passed as the result of litigation instituted by members of the legal profession whose oppressive conduct had from time to time swallowed a great portion of his income, which should have been used for other purposes, and some hundreds of which has gone into their own pockets. The true source of this indictment, claimed Champneys, was the hope entertained by Broderip and Co. that by his conviction they would succeed in an application to the Chancellor to have him removed as a member of the commission for peace, (magistrate), a situation that he had held for the county of Somerset and two other counties for 25 years.

He went on to say that he trusted that His Honour would enquire a little further into the case before attending to such an application since he was not unknown to him, having had the honour attending him as sheriff of the county and of receiving his thanks for the manner in which he had discharged the duty of his office. Not only had he the honour of being known as a man of integrity and fortune, his family had also borne that character for seven centuries. He denied the whole of the charge and insisted that the officers had been guilty of the assault and that what he did was nothing more than was required to repel their insolence.

Thomas Champney's co-defendants swore positively that the officers had entered the house after dark when both were excessively drunk and extremely rude, one so much so that he could barely sit on his horse. They had forced their way into the dining room where gold and silver plate stood on the sideboard totalling 40 times the value to be levied. The defence also stated that there was no such article as a settle in the house nor was there a bridge within half a mile of the property, which was surely untrue as there was a bridge not far from the house constructed in about 1800 by Thomas himself and giving access to the church, which still serves that purpose today. The two officers had sworn that one had fallen asleep in the settle, hardly the action of a sober man on duty, and they had both sworn that White was hauled over the bridge and threatened to be drowned in the pond.

Champneys' overlong justifications and recitals of his heritage probably didn't go down too well with the jury; all three were found guilty but released on bail to attend the court of King's Bench during the next term for sentencing. The defendants put in an application for a new trial immediately.

The old house & courtyard shortly before demolition. (M McGarvie)

Ralph Crozier, it seems, did not take his place in the dock. Since the summer of 1814 Crozier, who had for some years been one of Champneys most trusted servants and described by him as 'the head of my establishment' had been feeling deeply affronted. Champneys explained that he had received a transfer of indentures of apprenticeship for a lad of eight years named John West, one of his co-defendants, whose master was imprisoned for debt. West was set to work in the stables but quickly transferred to the house as was quite common but caused 'considerable jealousy to the upper servant Crozier'. Champneys continues,

> In the summer of 1814 I received an anonymous letter respecting this young man which led me to watch more narrowly his conduct. In the winter following I was thunderstruck to find in my letterbox another letter directed to me of a most equivocal description.[3]

West too received letters of the 'most insidious and aggravated description'. More letters of a similar nature followed and Champneys made an application to the magistrates at Bow Street who after much exertion traced the letters to a clerk named Simeon Gowen employed by an attorney at Lincolns Inn. Gowen was arrested and made and signed a full confession saying that he had been employed by Ralph Crozier to conduct this correspondence. According to Champneys, Gowen fell to the ground in an apoplectic fit from which he never recovered, expiring shortly afterwards, although this was disputed by others, Messiter claiming that he lived for another 14 months. .

Crozier was dismissed in February 1815, and according to Champneys, disappeared – although others claimed that he was still around. It seems odd that he should be so upset, but possibly there is more to the matter. Is it possible that West was replacing Crozier in Champneys' affections as well as his household duties? This poisoned pen campaign was quite possibly what lay behind the rumours of Champneys' sexual inclinations which began to circulate at that time. Did the rumourmongering arise from Crozier's campaign which was then taken up by the Messiters some years later, building upon a foundation of lies for his own ends? Or was Champneys in truth bisexual? (Years later George Messiter in a riposte to Champneys' accusation of him tampering with witnesses refers to West, 'Is he not the same person who had part of his ear bitten off and asserted that it was done by his Master?')[4]

The defendants had been busy collecting affidavits in support of a new trial and the court reassembled at Westminster Hall on 27 December 1815. They produced 18 signed statements from local people supporting the case that the two bailiffs had been drinking heavily throughout that day from 9am until 11 at night. (Though how this is squared with them being at Orchardleigh at 6.00pm is not explained – did they return to the pub after the altercation?). Crozier had not been seen since his dismissal over the letters scandal. Champneys addressed their lordships in what was described as a manly, nervous and pathetic speech solemnly declaring his innocence and appealing on behalf of his servants, stating that they were only doing their duty in protecting their master. The Chief Justice, Lord Ellenborough, directed that an indictment should be preferred against White and Baker and referred Champneys' convictions back to the Assize Court. 'Mr Champneys then bowed and left the court attended by a number of noblemen and gentlemen who had accompanied him, his cause having created much fascination in the higher circles'. White's trial took place in April and he was convicted, which removed the threat of imprisonment that had been hanging over Champneys and his servants. It was a narrow escape. Former stable boy John West is listed as gamekeeper for Orchardleigh, Frome, and Lullington, with 'lands in Marston Bigot', employed by Thomas Champneys during September 1816 and presumably beyond.

~~~

THE EARLY NINETEENTH century was a time of great poverty and discontent in Frome. There were riots over the price of food, principally bread and potatoes. Unemployment was rife due in part to the introduction of power looms taking away jobs and the general decline of the cloth industry, owing to competition from abroad and the better organised factories in the northern counties. During one disturbance in 1813 the riot act was read and four rioters prosecuted for assaulting the magistrates.

In the summer of 1816 what was to become known as the 'Battle of Frome' took place over 'an advance in the price of potatoes' by five pence
~~~

per peck due in part to the dreadful weather which destroyed the crop and gave rise to that year being known as 'The Year Without a Summer'. Press reports put the figure involved in this as rising to up to 3000 people, during which time Lieut. Colonel Wickham received a severe wound to the head, causing him to be removed from the scene along with seven or eight of the cavalry similarly wounded or bruised, and with one horse having its eye knocked out. Attempts were made to destroy the factory of Messrs. Sheppard but in this they were unsuccessful. Order was eventually restored by the arrival of a detachment of dragoons from Bruton.

In charge of the North Somerset Yeomanry, as it had become, on that occasion was Champneys' old adversary from the poaching case of 1805, Captain Richard B Thornhill. He was much put out by the accusation that his troop had been repulsed by the rioters and only saved by the arrival of the Bruton detachment. According to an eyewitness account Champneys arrived in the middle of the disturbance at about 10.00pm and spoke to the rioters asking them what they wanted, to which they replied that they wanted three of their arrested number released. Champneys then interviewed the men in question and finding that the charges were trivial ordered them to be set free, upon which the whole of the people dispersed.[5]

~~~

THERE ARE SOME reports of Champneys' many years as a magistrate but records were not kept as a matter of course and anything we do have comes from newspaper reports or contemporary diaries. On 4 September 1814 two boys were convicted of robbing a garden of fruit and he fined them two guineas with costs, or in default of payment within 48 hours they were ordered to be whipped by the constable.

In October 1816 he committed a Joel Wingrove aged 47 for trial for obtaining over £100 worth of yarn under false pretences, which must have gone against the grain, as the goods had been stolen from the Sheppard family with whom he was not on the best of terms and never would be. Wingrove received 18 months and was fined 1/- at the assize court

During this period, he was still making regular visits to London to attend fashionable balls or court hearings sometimes staying at the
~~~

Saint Petersburg Hotel in Dover Street with his wife.

In March 1817 Champneys presented a petition to the Prince Regent signed by upwards of 30,000 people covering Somerset, Gloucestershire and Wiltshire, asking for some restrictions upon the use of gig mills and shearing frames which would put many thousands of people out of work. This was received by his Royal Highness 'with most gracious and distinguished condensation'. In September of 1817 he took part in a public meeting at the George Hotel in Frome to consider establishing a savings bank for the general population of the town. Also behind the scheme were The Marquis of Bath and Lord Cork. The meeting was described as more respectable than numerous but nonetheless a committee was appointed and the meeting considered a great success.

There are some later reports of his time as a magistrate thanks to a diary kept by Frome's constable with whom he seems to have got on well enough. Isaac Gregory described Champneys as being 'very polite to me and paid some high compliments on fulfilling the office of constable so well...' However, there was one notable occasion in December 1817 when Gregory was called to the Eagle pub to sort out a Mr Biggs of Mells who was getting very agitated over some figs. Biggs refused to calm down and go home so Gregory grabbed hold of him with the help of the watchman and dragged him towards the guard house. Biggs struck Gregory a mighty blow to the face which almost floored him, and tried to escape. Gregory was furious at such treatment and determined to have him sent to prison. The following morning he was taken to Orchardleigh to appear before Champneys,

> Mr Champneys was in his park and said that we must take him back and bring him up again tomorrow for he would not give up his amusement. I told him that the prisoner was at his house and everything was ready for his signature but nothing would do, and I was obliged to return the following day extremely mortified at the injustice of a justice.

Biggs was very contrite and his wife turned up in tears begging forgiveness. Gregory was so annoyed by Champneys' 'shameful treatment' at Orchardleigh on the previous day that he withdrew the prosecution after recovering his expenses and the prisoner making a public apology, via a handbill which read: -

> Caution to Drunkards – Whereas I, James Biggs, labourer, did, on the night of the 10th violently assault Mr Isaac Gregory while in the execution of his duty and did, while in a state of intoxication, give him a violent blow on the face for which he has commenced action against me, that I may be punished with the utmost severity of the law, but in consequence of my publicly acknowledging my offence and begging for mercy and in compassion to my wife and child, has withdrawn the prosecution against me. I hope it will be a caution to me and all drunkards not to interrupt the peace officers in execution of their duty. Witness my hand in the presence of T S Champneys at Orchardleigh 12 December 1817'[6]

In January 1818 Queen Charlotte, wife of the declining George III announced her intention to spend a fortnight in Brighton, and upon her return to visit the homes of the Duke of Beaufort, the Marquis of Bath and Mr Champneys. An interesting addition to this announcement states that, 'The Queen's going to Bath and her Majesty's return from thence are utterly unknown to the King, and cannot of course, have given occasion to any irritation in his Majesty's mind, as has been erroneously reported.' That same month the larder at Orchardleigh was broken into and robbed of its contents. viz. a quarter, a saddle, two legs, two shoulders, two necks, and nine breasts of mutton, two sirloins and a piece of beef; a hindquarter, neck and breast of house lamb, a loin of veal, two sweetbreads, several pieces of pork, a turkey, a goose, a hare, five rabbits, several snipes, wildfowl etc. If her majesty did turn up it is to be hoped that she didn't bring too many people with her! As though losing his larder wasn't bad enough, severe storms uprooted a large number of trees on his estate during the same period. Whether her majesty ever called at Orchardleigh is not known but she died in November of the same year.

That April Thomas and his wife Charlotte attended the theatre in Bath to see the six-year-old infant prodigy Miss Clara Fisher with her troop of Lilliputians. During the same period, he contributed one guinea, as did Mrs Champneys, to the collection for a public monument to the memory of the late Princess Charlotte of Wales, organised by The Cenotaph Committee. Thomas was in charge of collecting from the Frome area and received contributions from well over 150 Frome notables – friend and foe alike, most contributing a guinea. The pair also attended a splendid ball and supper at the house of a Mrs Bethell in Grosvenor Place, London during May.

In June of 1818 Thomas Champneys was 49 years of age and according to one small mention in a London newspaper lent his support to the campaign of William Beckford, the 58-year-old Whig MP, for the tiny Wiltshire seat of Hindon near his mansion of Fonthill, a mere 20 miles from Orchardleigh. Beckford had held the seat briefly in 1790 and then again from 1806 to 1820. He was one of the most fascinating characters of the period whose predilections and eccentricities are far too well known to need much repetition here. Suffice it to say that his enthusiasm and ingenuity in disposing of a vast fortune, as well as his love of collecting and flamboyant display not just paralleled, but exceeded that of Champneys by a country mile. There is no evidence that they knew each other well or even met face to face, but reports of important society balls in London show the Champneys and a man recorded simply as 'Beckford' in attendance during the 1801-1808 seasons. They both owned large estates at home and also in Jamaica, so it would be strange indeed if they did not know each other to some degree, despite Beckford's frequent trips to the continent. [7]

Earl of Sefton.
Mr. Beckford, of Fonthill, will be again returned for Hindon, in Wiltshire, without opposition; and we understand Thomas Swymmer Champneys, Esq. of Orchardleigh, near Frome, has commenced an active canvass, as his colleague; and, possessing the interest of Mr. Beckford, entertains no doubt of success.

Announcement in the Morning Post of June 19 1818

Like many constituencies of the time Hindon was notoriously corrupt and although Beckford would allegedly give promises to supporters rather than take bribes it was still illegal, though he stood on a reforming ticket. Despite gaining a few seats the Whigs were defeated and the Tories retained control of the country.

Back in the courts, in November 1818 he sentenced three drunken lads from Corsley to a £5 fine and a signed public apology after they disrupted a church service. They had already spent two nights in the guard house and this was thought to have been enough.

Not everything in the courtroom went his way. In the early part of 1819 he had fined a collector of tolls 40 shillings for demanding a toll for a cart passing from one part of a farm to another conveying pails of milk, which he considered to be implements of husbandry and therefore exempt under the act. It seems that Champneys was alone on the bench when he convicted the toll keeper and hearing of the impending appeal his fellow magistrates held a meeting and agreed with his decision unanimously. Nonetheless the toll keeper won his appeal on the bizarre grounds that there was a difference between the transportation of empty pails which could be considered implements and the transportation of full ones due to an increase in weight which would subject them to the toll.

Periodically the constables of Frome would carry out raids on the local shopkeepers and publicans to inspect their weights and measures. In May 1819 300 deficient weights were seized in the town and Champneys and his fellow magistrate John Sainsbury sat from 11.00am until 7.00pm going through nearly 70 of these cases. Many of the individuals had from 10 to 15 illegal weights in their possession and had to pay the full penalty with costs; more than 100 convictions were recorded.

Aside from his work as a magistrate Champneys was involved in an organisation formed to consider the best means of 'providing employment for the labouring poor'. A meeting was held at the George Hotel in late September 1819 and presided over by the Marquis of Bath. It 'was fully entered into by that active and patriotic magistrate Mr Champneys who in a speech of considerable length, full of feeling and information stated that,

> ... such was the patient orderly and well-conditioned conduct of the lower orders within the division of Frome under deprivations as unforeseen as severe, that his confidence in their general character and disposition led him believe that all the subtle sophistry of the most sophisticated demagogue would not shake their loyalty and good sense. But, he observed an Englishman will not, should not starve, and God forbid! there ever should be wanting in this happy land of inherent rights and equal laws fit and proper men by birth and education to maintain and enforce those rights and privileges to the security and protection of the meanest pauper of the land who may think fit to claim them.

The meeting was attended by the Earl of Cork, Rev J M Rogers, Charles Knatchbull, Rev J Algar, Rev J P L. Fenwick, Rev S H Cassan as well as Messrs Sheppard, Tom Bunn and others.

By their second meeting, a few weeks later and chaired by Champneys, they had compiled their first report and collected £1200, £600 of which was raised by subscription and the remainder matched from the Poor Rates. Some of the money was to be used to pay a premium to farmers in the parish or within four miles of it who would agree to employ any number of the labouring poor of the parish of Frome. Other sums will be used to employ men to work on improving the roads. At a special vestry meeting it was agreed, somewhat bizarrely, that further sums will be used to give encouragement under the sanction of the government, to those wishing to emigrate to the Cape of Good Hope. It was further recommended that several publicans within the parish should pay strict and unvaried attention to the orders of the magistrates respecting the time for closing their houses at night and that persons requiring parochial relief who have families to support should abstain from frequenting public houses. The committee met weekly and seemed very much under Champney's control and direction. By their 12th meeting in mid-December out of 250 labourers that given their names at the start it was now proving difficult to find 10 men to fulfil various roles.

At one of their meetings in January 1820 they were joined by William Davis Bayly described as of Frome and the Inner Temple, a local solicitor working for his father in London. Bayly had written a book entitled *The State of the Poor and Working Classes Considered, with practical plans for improving their condition in society and superseding the present system of compulsory assessment.*[8] He introduced this to the assembled company in a 'long and lucid explanation of his system during which he read many pages from the pamphlet recently published by him to which they listened with great attention until a late hour before adjourning for a fortnight in order to read the pamphlet and consider its contents'. By the beginning of 1820 they were able to say that not one individual had applied for work and been sent away empty-handed for the last 17 weeks, also the sum of £130 had been collected in the last 10 days to supply the poor with coal and soup. A further £200 had been advanced by the turnpike commissioners towards completing a road for which the Poor Committee had voted £300.

Another example of his generosity despite his own crippling debts was the donation of several hundred pounds for the purchase of the leasehold interest in two acres of ground for the site and burial ground of Christchurch which opened its doors as a 'free church', which meant that no one had to pay rent for a pew, in September1818 with a procession of 50 clergymen led by The Marquis of Bath, The Earl of Cork and Thomas Champneys followed by an immense concourse of people despite terrible weather. [9]

[1] *The Complete Farrier* 1816
[2] ibid
[3] Messiter 1822 p75
[4] *Report of the Trial of a Indictment...* 1822
[5] John Allen in Cobbett's Political Register 1816-07-20
[6] McGarvie *Crime and Punishment in Regency Frome* FSLS 1984
[7] 1785 Mowl p129 and various dates
[8] available free on Google Books
[9] Gill *Experiences.....* 2003 p 418

8
1820 KIDNAP AND IMPRISONMENT

FOR THOMAS CHAMPNEYS life was about to take a turn for the worse. By 1820 he, '...who had long been a man of the first fashion in the county, who was a magistrate and who had once been a man of opulence, had, by a course of imprudence, become involved in a most distressing state of embarrassment'. Despite all his attempts to ignore the situation Thomas was approaching bankruptcy.

In the spring of 1817 he had become indebted to Moses Abraham, a silversmith and watchmaker of Frome, for the sum of £630. Abraham was demanding repayment and when Champneys told him that he was unable to pay he mentioned that Nathaniel Messiter a local banker and wool merchant had the sum of £800 which he would be able to lend on reasonable terms. Champneys financial problems were well known and it can be safely assumed that it was equally well-known that he was not the most careful of men in the district where money was concerned.

In December of 1819 reports had begun to circulate around town that goods were to be seized from Champney's house at Orchardleigh for the benefit of his creditors and that a sale of his effects was about to be advertised. A meeting in his support made up of local businessmen and worthies, that Champneys described as 'totally unsolicited', took place at the George Inn and 37 of those attending put their names to securities totalling £3,500 which they deposited at the bank to Mr Champneys order. The next time he rode into Frome to sit as a magistrate he was met on the road by 'hundreds of local people, his horses were taken from his carriage and he was drawn into town amidst the ringing of bells and universal acclamations'.[1] With Champneys now desperate for money to pay off some debts and prevent another invasion of his estate he met Messiter at Orchardleigh and terms were discussed. Champneys agreed to pay Messiter £70 legal fees and £100 in interest on a loan of £800 for two months. When the trustees of the Orchardleigh estate became aware of the terms of the agreement they were outraged and threatened proceedings against Messiter for usury or charging an extortionate amount of interest, a conviction for which would have ruined Messiter's business and reputation. Messiter panicked and attempted to repay part of his fee by returning to Orchardleigh and leaving £50 on Champney's table. This was refused and from that time Champneys dates 'a deep-rooted malice in the defendant'. Determined to get the upper hand and achieve some sort of bargaining power against being taken to court, Messiter went around town and purchased all the small debts and securities that he could find with Champney's name attached to them in order to bring legal actions for debt and run up costs against him.

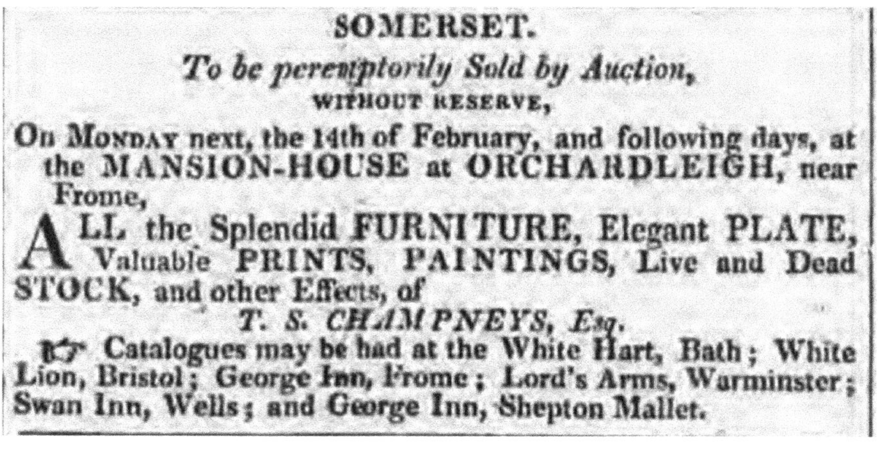

SOMERSET.

To be peremptorily Sold by Auction,

WITHOUT RESERVE,

On MONDAY next, the 14th of February, and following days, at the MANSION-HOUSE at ORCHARDLEIGH, near Frome,

ALL the Splendid FURNITURE, Elegant PLATE, Valuable PRINTS, PAINTINGS, Live and Dead STOCK, and other Effects, of

T. S. CHAMPNEYS, Esq.

☞ Catalogues may be had at the White Hart, Bath; White Lion, Bristol; George Inn, Frome; Lord's Arms, Warminster; Swan Inn, Wells; and George Inn, Shepton Mallet.

The Bristol Mercury 7 February 1820

On 1 January 1820 an advertisement appeared in the local papers advertising that the contents of Champneys mansion were to be put up for auction. The sale was postponed until the following week despite notices in some papers saying that it had been abandoned, possibly put about by Champneys himself or his supporters.

Frome resident John Allen Giles, a polymath who translated Greek and Latin classics into English, kept a detailed diary of his time in Frome and describes the scene prior to auction,

> Sir Thomas... 'was constantly in debt and got into what other men would call trouble for want of money to pay his debts; but Sir Thomas was wonderfully insensible to trouble on that head. At last an execution was put into his house at Orchardleigh and although this was staved off by the mediation of my father and others the whole property came to the hammer about three months later and the whole affair caused much amusement to all our school boys. We walked over every day whilst the public were admitted to inspect the things and carried on all manner of larks. There was a complete set of masquerade dresses suited for hobgoblins and ghosts with a dragon and other respectable animals from terra incognita and some of the men-servants were dressed up in these costumes that visitors might see and appreciate them before the sale. There was moreover a splendid collection of paintings but these were transferred for sale to Frome seeing that purchasers both dealers and private gentleman would come from distant places and could more readily find board and lodging in the town without the trouble and cost of going two or three miles further into the country. The paintings were therefore sold in Frome by Mr Harold auctioneer who now and then amused the company by his mis pronunciation. I think the library was also sold in Frome and I believe it was there that my father bought for me two most splendid volumes bound in gold and Morocco and illustrated with the most beautiful coloured prints, Hervey's Mediations. [2]

~~~

CHAMPNEYS HAD A number of writs against him for various amounts and when he was taken to court Nathaniel Messiter and William Chislett, a local attorney who had also been against him in the church sexton dispute, stood bail or surety for him in the sum of £1,000. In those days the sureties had a lot of power over the bailee and were they to withdraw, the defendant could be arrested and placed in prison while replacements were found or the debts were repaid – they had the right to have the debtor arrested whenever they pleased, on any day and at all times. Normally, of course, the person standing bail would be either a relative, close friend or supervisor of those in danger of imprisonment but in this case nothing could be further from the truth. Along with the King's Bench writs there were two warrants for his immediate arrest
~~~

and imprisonment concerning a creditor named Middleton to whom he owed almost £600. This was probably John Middleton or his father who ran a carriage service to London and was part of the Frome infantry company formed in in 1803. The warrants were issued by the Sheriff of Somerset and were only enforceable within that county.

Champneys decided to lie low at his father's estate in Hampshire avoiding the auction at his house and waiting until the bailiffs had gone.[3] Possibly he went there to ask his father for money but once the date of the auction had passed he made his way via the Black Dog Inn, Standerwick Common in Wiltshire on the border with Somerset. His plan was to stay just outside Somerset while he found a way of settling the outstanding amount through his Bath solicitor Mr Evill and avoid arrest before returning home. He arrived there on 24 February ten days after the auctioneer's raid on his house and ordered dinner and a room for the night. Word of his return had obviously got out and that evening Nathaniel Messiter along with his two sons George, an attorney, and John, a wool sorter, made their way to the inn to apprehend him.

Arriving at the inn and without waiting for any announcement George Messiter followed Champneys' servant George Higgins to the inn's parlour where Champneys was writing. Being a 'gentleman of polished manners' he received them civilly but was soon to discover that their intentions were anything but honourable. The Messiters' informed him that they intended to take him to London to have his bail discharged at the King's Bench and to which he had no choice but to agree. He was denied the dinner that was prepared and waiting for him and told that they would dine at the Angel in Warminster. Outnumbered and knowing that the law was on their side, he had no alternative but to go along with them.

Champneys was aware of two Somerset *'capias ad satisfaciendum'*[4] warrants out against him which were only valid within Somerset but if served would have meant his immediate imprisonment by the local sheriff until the debt was paid in full. He received a promise from George Messiter that these would not be enforced. Messiter even went as far as showing that he had the two writs in his pocket but swore that he would not execute them, claiming that they were taking him to London via Warminster where he would appear before the King's Bench. Contemporary accounts detail the series of events: -

On this understanding Champneys entered the chaise which had been procured from Frome and had the additional accommodation of a dickey box.[5] It had been sent for after the arrival of the Messiters at the Black Dog and the driver was told on his arrival to set his horses heads towards Warminster, but as soon as Mr Champneys was secured, to drive as hard as possible for two miles on the Frome road. Mr Champneys was accompanied in the carriage by Thomas Ivey, the sheriff's officer. George Messiter mounted the dickey box, John Messiter performed the office of footman and their father Nathaniel Messiter that of outrider on horseback. In this way all proceeded quietly until the horses were suddenly turned around to the Frome road, and the plaintiff, seeing how he had been deceived put his hand upon George Messiter's shoulder and said "You traitor you have entrapped and deceived me; how can I take your word again as a gentleman?" Champneys entreated Messiter to return: but his plea met with no other reply than the appearance of a drawn dagger and a threat of applying its powers.

Maddened, the plaintiff reached across to the door next to the bailiff and in so doing kicked a box containing his possessions against it causing it to fall into the road and smash. The next state in which the plaintiff was found was that of being half out of the carriage exclaiming 'Murder!' The horses were by now in full gallop and he was dragged till the cries of the bailiff who did not lease his hold, added to those of the plaintiff, caused the carriage to stop. When it had done so the bailiff loosened his fingers and Champneys fell to the ground being immediately seized by John and George Messiter and a few moments later Nathaniel Messiter the father rode back and without provocation struck the plaintiff a violent blow with a black thorn cudgel on his head which caused him to stagger but fortunately only demolished his hat. Force was then used to drag the plaintiff once more to the carriage, but he absolutely refused unless his box, in which was a valuable gold watch and £50 in cash was given to him. This Nathaniel Messiter refused crying, "Drag him along, the scoundrel, drag him along, I have pistols and will use them!"

The more humane bailiff, Mr Ivey advised Mr Champneys to get into the carriage again upon being promised that his box should be restored. Champneys got in and was fixed between Ivey, and John Messiter who was promoted from the footboard and in this way the party travelled until they got within about half a mile of the county of Somerset where they were met by Sheriff Williamson, father in law to Ivey, who accosted them by inquiring if Squire Champneys was in the carriage? 'Oh yes,' replied George Messiter, 'he is here'. Sheriff Williamson, who had of course been part of the plot against the plaintiff and was waiting to arrest him, had received the warrants from George Messier at the Black Dog earlier in the evening unseen by Champneys. He proceeded to take the plaintiff in execution upon those very writs which George Messiter had vowed to God should not be executed as soon as they crossed over the county border. Mr Williamson then took the place of John Messiter and in this way the party arrived at the George Inn at Frome.

Mr Champneys, under these circumstances, was thrown into a violent fever and although there was no sign of violence upon his person he was confined to his bed for several days and required the attendance of a medical person, being bruised and hardly able to walk. During that time he was locked in his room at the George with Ivey and Williamson in a room adjoining. At the end of five days he was released from his bail upon his solicitor, Mr Evill [6] of Bath joining in a bond of indemnity to Nathaniel Messiter and was able to discharge the writs of *ca.sa.*

On the 29th he was released and returned to his home drawn in his carriage by the populace of Frome, the outstanding sum having been paid by the 'unsolicited assistance of a noble Marquess and many of his neighbours who had long known him'. After taking legal advice he issued a writ against Messiter on 22 March alleging that the Messiters and their servant were guilty of assault, false imprisonment and trespass.[7] Sometime previous to this on 6 March Messiter issued a statement by way of a pre-emptive strike,

To the Inhabitants of Frome
Mr Champneys has stated that on taking him into custody lately, I drew a dagger and stabbed at him, I assert this to be false, and at the whole account given by him of that transaction a gross misstatement. If I acted illegally in bringing Mr Champneys into Somersetshire, he has his remedy against me. Altho' Mr Champneys threatened me with pistols, insulted me by the grossest abuse, endeavoured to throw me out of the dickey under the wheels of the chaise, attacked and collr'd me

several times, I assert that no return was made to his assault on me, no violence used till he jumped out of the chaise, nor was any force then used beyond what was necessary to prevent his escape.

I had a dagger up my sleeve; when Mr Champneys tried to throw me under the wheels this came into my hand; so soon as he released me I put it into my greatcoat pocket and did not again take it thence till I reached home. Mr Champneys saw me put something into my coat pocket and exclaimed that I had a pistol he persisted in saying that I had a pistol till Thomas Ivey told him it was a dagger. When or why Mr Champneys made the hole in his coat he best knows.

I pledge myself for the truth of the statement.

GEO. MESSITER Frome March 6 1820[8]

Mr Champneys 'had his remedy' indeed and the case opened at the Wiltshire Summer Assizes in Salisbury on 25 July 1820 before Mr Justice Burrough and a special jury. According to the *Bristol Mirror* the court was 'crowded to excess and many of the nobility and gentry of Wiltshire and Somerset were present'.

Sergeant Pell addressed the court on behalf of the plaintiff, Thomas Champneys, describing his client as 'the son of a baronet living in Somerset in that degree of fashion and consideration which has long given him much attention on the part of the public; I might also add that he is a gentleman pretty much marked by imprudence as well as misfortune'.

Bailiff Ivey, Higgins and the coachman gave evidence as to the facts as they knew them and the Messiters claimed that they were doing no more than they were warranted to do in preventing the plaintiff's escape from lawful custody and that in standing bail they had the right to render a defendant whenever and wherever they chose.

During the cross-examination of George Higgins Mr Stephen Gaselee for the defence, attempted to prove that Champneys kept a large drum just outside the house which was used to summon tenants and employees to the house when under attack by bailiffs – though what possible bearing this had on the case is far from clear! It was strongly denied by Higgins who claimed that his master sometimes assembled a band of music which make use of it.

Sergeant Pell's concluding appeal on the behalf of Mr Champneys created strong sensations in his favour and 'left not many dry eyes in the court'. As defendants the Messiters could not be called to give evidence as the law stood at that time and had to speak through their legal representatives. The trial lasted a mere seven hours and although the court reporter was unable to hear the judge's words in summing up he heard enough to conclude that it was strongly in Champneys favour. The jury took only 10 minutes to find the Messiters guilty. Champneys had won his case and the jury awarded damages of £700, a little shy of the £5,000 he had asked for, but a victory none the less.

In an attempt to justify himself George Messiter wrote to the local papers a few days later. He rehearsed the arguments that he had used in court and claimed that he had provided himself with the dagger solely to prevent violence by showing that he was not unprepared. This was after hearing stories of Champneys's conduct when threatened with having his goods removed last February, during which time he claimed that 200 men could be brought over at the drop of a hat to prevent the removal of his goods, and that he kept ready firearms to shoot anyone who tried to take his person.

This whole episode can be seen as nothing more than an attempt at revenge upon Champneys by the Messiters and Frome's professional class for all the personal animosity that had gone on over the previous years – dating back to the volunteers' dispute of 1803, and the battle was far from over.

[1] *Slander* p 5
[2] YB volume 18 p 37
[3] *Slander* p 5
[4] This is executed by arresting the defendant, and keeping him in custody until he is able give security for the payment of the debt, or upon his promise to return into custody again before the return day. The writ is, in common language, called a ca. sa.
[5] An external seat on a coach normally used by a servant.
[6] Evill and Else of Wood Street, Bath
[7] *Slander* p 6
[8] Frome Museum

9
UNNATURAL PRACTICES? AUGUST 1820

DESPITE LOSING THE case George Messiter showed no signs of giving up his vendetta – far from it. Whether he thought that by damaging Champneys' reputation so badly the events at the Black Dog would be quietly dropped or that any action for usury would not be proceeded with is not known, but shortly after he was charged with the assault in March of 1820 Messiter began his campaign of slander. Malicious gossip about Champneys making sexual advances towards John Cuzner, one of his tenants, a fuller who lived at Lullington, began to circulate around the town. If it could have been proven that such activity had taken place Champneys could have been facing the death penalty. The Buggery Act of 1533 was still in force, a situation which existed until 1861. Fifty men were executed between 1805 and 1832 and the last pair were hanged in 1835. To accuse someone of sodomy was a well-known tactic to use against one's enemies at that time, an allegation notoriously hard to prove – but equally hard to disprove, with the advantage that mud sticks and membership of the aristocracy was no defence. Men feared the blackmailers because their threats could lead to indelible disgrace, loss of reputation as well as the social and financial ruin.

Champneys took Messiter to court at the King's Bench sitting in Wells before Mr Justice Burrough and a special jury on 11 August 1820 charging him with slander. The prosecutor Sergeant-at-Law Albert Pell gave a brief outline of his client's history and position in society – being careful to emphasise that,

> He was married nearly 29 years since, to the sister of the present Sir Thomas Mostyn MP for the county of Flint – one of the most amiable, accomplished, and beautiful of women; he has lived with her during

> the whole of that long period in one uninterrupted course of connubial happiness and has not been absent from her one month in the aggregate.[1]

Pell explained that that the plaintiff had faced many financial difficulties in recent years and many had sought to take advantage of the situation, one of these was the defendant George Messiter. He described the events at the Black Dog some months before as previously outlined and continued with his opening address,

> Gentlemen, the case you are to try is this, – you are to decide whether England is worth living in or not; for if, after the proof of the facts which I shall lay before you today, anything short of the heaviest damages are given that can be given upon such an occasion, in my judgement in this country is no longer worth remaining in... I will leave the case with you; I shall only state that the damages declaration are stated at £10,000... and I think that will be a guide to your verdict as to the extent of damages that are to be given.[2]

Pell concluded his opening remarks by saying how remarkable it would be that if a man of Mr Champneys' standing *was* guilty of such activities that he could continue to serve on special juries, sit as a magistrate and be summoned as a grand juror with its being widely known that he was a sodomite. The court then proceeded to consider the evidence.

On the 22 March 1820 George Messiter initiated a conversation with Charles Vincent, landlord of the Waggon and Horses in Frome. He asked Vincent if he had heard the report about Mr Champneys to which Vincent replied that he had only heard what was common knowledge – that more goods were to be seized from his house. Messiter replied that,

> It is something a great deal worse than that or anything else that has happened or can happen respecting his money matters.
>
> It is reported that Mr Champneys has been buggering.
>
> God bless me! it never can be true! where did you get the information?
>
> I heard it from one of Mr Champneys' tenants his name is Cuzner and who has been in prison on his account'.

Vincent said that he hoped it was not true, to which Messiter replied that from what Cuzner had said it was all too plain. Vincent gave evidence at the hearing and when pressed by Mr Justice Burrough to give more details of the conversation he gave evidence as follows,

> He, (Messiter) said that Mr Champneys was in his room with Cuzner and that he had taken very indecent liberties with him, such as pulling his apron to one side and began feeling about his person and put his hand into his breeches and then unbuttoned his own, and forced Cuzner's hand into his small clothes.[3]

Messiter was next in conversation with a Mr Charles Willoughby, a dealer in tea, wines, spirits and banking who also lived in Frome. In the early part of March Champneys was to sit as a magistrate in the case of a man charged with sodomy; Messiter opened his conversation with Willoughby by saying what a singular thing it was that he should be trying a case of this nature and when asked why, he again brought up his allegations against Champneys' activities saying,

> I can prove it in many instances with half a dozen people or more. I can prove him in the very fact; or rather I can bring persons to prove it or even bring a person to swear it.

Messiter went on to state that he had been hearing too many similar reports all over the town and neighbourhood for the previous two to three weeks. Now came a crucial piece of evidence, Willoughby was asked if he had ever heard such rumours about Champneys previously. He replied that he had about four years before when somebody had asked him if he had heard about Mr Champneys being *at the Westbury work*.[4] This, it will be remembered, is around the time that Crozier initiated his campaign of letter writing.

William Davis, a clerk to the magistrates, was called as a witness and stated that the man's case of attempting to commit an unnatural crime with another man was heard by Mr Champneys at Orchardleigh in April and that he removed the case to Frome where it was heard by a number of magistrates. The man was committed to the Assizes and eventually convicted.

The next witness was a millwright named Henry Wheeler whom Messiter had engaged in conversation in the Market Place on or around the 15 March, claiming that he could bring forward a very respectable witness who had caught Champneys in the very act of sodomy. Not content with spreading rumours, the prosecution alleged, Messiter had set about finding some people whom he could pressure into becoming witnesses.

Next, he called Robert Fry, who described himself as an agent who was selling goods on commission in London during May and asked him whether Mr Champneys had not taken liberties with his son William, to which Fry replied, 'no, not to my knowledge'. Messiter said that he knew it to be true and that you might as well come forward and that you shall not want for money. Fry said that his son was not to be bribed and asked Messiter how he had obtained the information, to which he replied that he had it from Mrs Crook the mason's wife at Lullington. Messiter finished by saying, 'you had better tell me and I will do you all the good in my power!' By this time Messiter knew about the Champneys impending court case against him and was looking to recruit witnesses in his defence.[5]

Robert Fry was followed by his son James, a wool spinner who lived at Lullington and claimed that Messiter had told him that a Mr Cox, (presumably his uncle Richard) in London, was going to supply Mr Champneys with money to bring an action against him. He said in the first place that he could prove that it was not him that had put it about, and in the second place he could prove that it was true. 'He wanted to know what attempt Champneys had made with me. I told him there was none and that I never saw anything of the kind with him in my life. He said that if I came forward for him I would never want for money'.

Cuzner, the supposed main complainant was not called by either side; he had been committed to prison by Champneys on an entirely different matter and his testimony might have been thought of as seeking revenge. It might also have been asked of him why he did not immediately report Champneys for his actions.

That concluded the witnesses for the prosecution.

Mr Gaselee for the defence called no witnesses as to the fact of the act which, he explained, by saying that anyone who appeared to prove that the offences had taken place could lay themselves open to involvement in a capital offence. He gave a long speech about how a finding of guilt would destroy the defendant's income, career and reputation and as though anticipating the verdict, he spent some time in explaining to the jury that for the plaintiff to be awarded anything near the amount of damages demanded by the prosecution his life and character would have to be without fault, which would not be the case if he had been addicted to 'unnatural propensities' such as those alluded to by rumour four or more years before. Gaselee then called witnesses in Messiter's defence.

Mr Wheeler testified that he had heard the rumours in the middle of March, which is before the date given by Vincent, and stated further that he had immediately told other people of what was being said. Wheeler was a cousin of Samuel Wheeler, Champneys' gamekeeper; would he not, asked Gaselee, have told his cousin who would have then repeated the words to Mr Champneys?[6] And would not Champneys have brought this action upon them instead of Messiter? Also, Wheeler stated in evidence that if he had been on particularly friendly terms with the defendant for up to two years why was he chosen as the conduit for such a rumour?

When Vincent asked Messiter if he thought that the allegations could be proved his reply was, 'No I hope not'. He stated at once that the story came from a cousin that he does not believe it to be true and hopes it cannot be proved. As soon as Champneys hears of the rumours he sends for Vincent who first contacts Messiter who advises him to, 'tell the whole story, tell all what I told you and tell him that I am ready to give up the author of the report if he thinks fit to trace it'. The obvious next course, claimed the defence, would be for Mr Champneys to demand an interview with the originator of the rumours but he does not do that, instead he brings actions against Mr Messiter.

Mr Willoughby is very precise about the date upon which he heard the rumours – 24 February at the Frome Fair – but the first time that Messiter is alleged to have said anything was 22 March according to Vincent, and in the middle of March according to Wheeler. We also have the evidence for Mr Davis who claims he also just heard such rumours four years ago. Messiter claimed that he sent a letter to Mr Champneys on the 4 April in the following terms,

> The foul report against you and which you suppose to have originated with me was circulated in Frome 10 days before I heard of it; this I state in justice to myself and in justice to you. I beg to observe, that I am willing, when called upon, to name the persons from whom I heard it which I presume is all that can be required of me'.[7] Mr Champneys denies ever having seen such a letter but Pell later admitted that there had been a letter which was now lost and the contents of which could not be known.

Towards the end of his remarks Gaselee made the following comments,

> I shall call before you a great number of witnesses, very respectable persons in almost every situation in life.... who will tell you that 10 years ago, 12 years ago, 5 years ago.... that they had for a period of 10 years downwards heard reports of the nature of that which is being circulated upon the present occasion, and that they had from time to time heard those reports.[8]

John French – Frome clothier – claims that he spoke to John Cuzner at the Bell public house in Frome, who was very agitated when Champneys' name was mentioned. Cuzner told French that once in Champneys' dressing room Champneys had attacked him with violence,

> .. by thrusting his hand into Cuzner's small clothes and handled him very indecently in the private parts. Champneys then exhibited his own private parts and compelled Cuzner to put his hand upon it. [9]

All this French told to Stephen Greenland, another Frome clothier, who then reported it to Messiter.

Dr Bush a surgeon claimed that he had first heard reports of Champneys having some unnatural propensities about six or seven years ago. He carried on normal relations with him until he heard about the affair of John Cuzner after which he had nothing more to do with him.

Mr Edmund Broderib who had known Champneys for many years was the next witness. 'Have you ever heard reports of Mr Champneys' propensities?' 'I have.' 'For how many years have you heard reports of that description?' 'Once about six years ago it was that he had been practising in that sort away with one of the servants.' 'Who did you hear it from?' 'One of the sheriff's officers said it was the common report in the house.' 'Was that about the time there was an indictment against Mr Champneys for assaulting the officer?' 'It was. I have heard similar reports since last March at about the time that Mr Champneys sale was going forward.'

George Sheppard, manufacturer, gave evidence that he had heard reports about five years ago that Mr Champneys was addicted to unnatural indelicacies and indecencies. 'I see him most Mondays when we have a Poor Committee.' The witness stated that he had not mentioned the rumours to Mr Champneys but had seen him working quite normally with other magistrates.

Sir John Cox Hippisley a magistrate who had known Champneys for between 20 to 30 years gave evidence that he had heard rumours for the last four to five years when they were quite common. 'I never told him of these reports, I have seen him quite often with Mrs Champneys. They seem to be on very good terms and I believe that she has always lived with him.' The witness believed that Mr Champneys was on the rules of the King's Bench and had heard that his wife was with him. The witness observed him moving in fashionable circles and with others of his station and had dined with him at the Bishop's Palace in Wells around four years ago. In cross-examination Mr Pell gave the opinion that the witness could not have believed the rumours or he would not have continued to associate with him.

The Rev John Methuen Rogers, magistrate, gave evidence that he had also known Champneys for between 20 and 30 years and that about four years ago Sir William A'Court first mentioned the rumours to him.

Rev Francis Skurray of Horningsham and incumbent of Lullington church stated that he had heard rumours six or seven years ago that Mr Champneys was addicted to unseemly conduct with respect to men. He continued that he had dined with him since first hearing the reports but had not mentioned them to him.

William Barter, a brewer in Frome, had known Mr Champneys for around 20 years and first heard reports that he was addicted to certain practices about 10 years ago and that some gentlemen in the neighbourhood were not intimate with him because of this.

This was the end of the defence witnesses.

Serjeant Pell explained to the court that he had been counsel for the Rev Ireland in the sexton's dispute many years before in opposition to Champneys and then gave his speech for the prosecution in the present case. His main thrust was that if any of the defence witnesses believed the rumours that they were hearing they should have had nothing further to do with Thomas Champneys. If they didn't believe them then surely it was their duty to inform him, if not as a friend, then surely as a long-standing associate, of what was being said about him. Mr Champneys might then have had the opportunity of vindicating his character from the infamous aspiration cast upon it. If Mr Champneys had been this infamous wretch was he a man to sit in judgement upon his fellow creatures? Pell continued his closing speech to the jury,

> Good God! Would I, if I knew that there was any man to sit in judgement upon the life of a fellow creature, if I had reason to believe that man was so infamous as to deserve to be an outcast in society, should I be discharging my duty in letting any man's life be put under the control and so be subject to his judgement?[10]
>
> He is now in personal confinement in consequence of his pecuniary distress. He has no friends but you and with such assistance as I could afford him....there is but one way in which he can receive help, and that is by your giving such a verdict, as I trust in this case you will give, more for the means, by that verdict, of showing your opinion that his character has been gravely injured than for the sake of any pecuniary compensation which he is to put in his pocket.[11]

Mr Justice Burrough in his summing up said that, 'there has been no attempt to prove the truth of the allegations, and that even if Messiter had heard reports he was not justified in saying that he knew them to be true or that he could prove them.' The case concluded with a victory for Champneys but he was only awarded £200.

It is important to remember that it was Messiter on trial for spreading slanderous rumours and not Champneys for the alleged offences. Rumours of Champneys' sexuality had started many years before but seem to have come to the fore during the poisoned pen case between Crosier and West, as a number of witnesses refer to having heard rumours four to five years previously. Any gossip before that seems to have been confined to the boundaries of Orchardleigh. Possibly Champneys could have brought similar charges against others months or longer before his case against Messiter, but such was the hatred between the two men that he could not resist an attack on his old enemy despite the publicity that this entailed.

[1] *Slander* p 3
[2] *Slander* p 7
[3] *Slander* p 18
[4] presumably a contemporary term for homosexual relations! Slander p 26
[5] *Slander* p 12
[6] *Slander* p 45
[7] *Slander* p 56
[8] *Slander* p 57
[9] *Slander* p 60
[10] *Slander* p 94
[11] *Slander* p 100

10
COURT AND THE KING'S BENCH RULES

During June and throughout August 1820 when Messiter's trial for slander took place, Champneys was confined 'within the rules of the King's Bench' in Southwark, South London. This consisted of an actual prison building in Belvedere Place, overcrowded and dirty like all prisons, but privately run so that inmates had to provide their own food and bedding. Often five or six hundred people were squeezed into two hundred and twenty-four tiny cells, most less than nine feet long. The better off prisoners could live in one of the eight 'state rooms' but those on the breadline lived by begging or on the charity of their fellows. Even within the prison itself there were facilities that make it sound like a pretty soft option as prisons went at that time. The yard had a coffee house, two pubs, butchers' stands, chandlers' shops and a surgery.

For the better class of debtor the prison operated a system of liberties, or Rules, as they were called, that allowed inmates to live in lodgings within an area about three miles in circumference around the main prison block Those sentenced were not supposed to stray beyond the boundaries of the Rules but enforcement was lax and when the Lord Chief Justice Ellenborough was applied to for an extension of the permitted area he replied gravely that he really could see no grounds for it since to his certain knowledge they already extended as far as the East Indies.

On some occasions there was an open-air market where hawkers of all kinds plied their wares along with racket grounds and fives courts. All this was of course dependent on how much money you or your supporters could provide, and seeing as most of those confined there were under its control until they could pay their debts there would not have been many who could afford such 'luxury'. Champneys lived, at least nominally, in West Square, which looks on the map to be just outside the area, but boundaries were rather relaxed and he was free to attend his frequent court appearances and any other business that needed his attention in the capital – presumably including the occasional masked ball or party. Frome historian J O Lewis writing in 1935 records that, 'I am told that once he got one of his tenants to take his place in the house in King's Bench while he went away,' but Lewis gives no source for this assertion.

In August 1820 the new king, George IV introduced a bill into Parliament known as the 'Pains and Penalties Bill' with the aim of

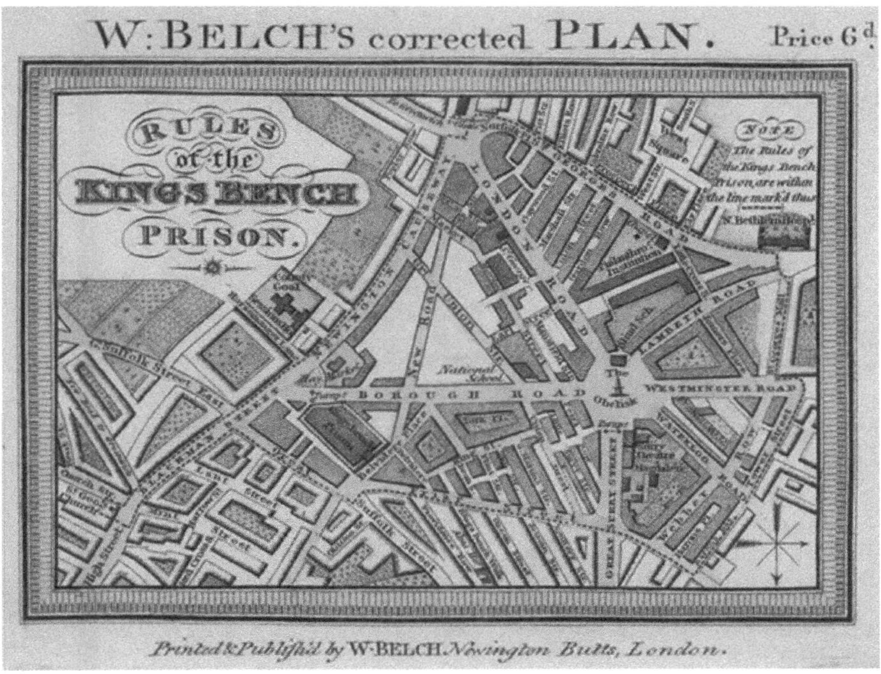

The 'Rules' of the King's Bench in 1830

dissolving his marriage to Queen Caroline. The pair despised each other and both had affairs and had lived apart for some time. Caroline insisted upon assuming her role as queen and with the simple solution adopted by his predecessor, Henry VIII, unavailable to him, George took her to court in the hope of proving her adultery, which was the only way to get the marriage dissolved. The debate in the House of Lords amounted to a trial of the queen for adultery with much salacious evidence being produced.

The King's Bench in the nineteenth century

The vote in the House resulted in a narrow victory for King George with a majority of only nine. A margin so narrow that it was not expected to pass through the Commons and the bill was withdrawn, which Caroline and her supporters considered a victory. There were great celebrations amongst the people; the debate had become political, with popular opinion siding with Caroline and signatures on petitions pledging support for her were organised by the radical leaders of the day, while those of a more conservative bent organised counter petitions in support of the king.

For once Champneys was in the latter camp but his banishment to London meant that he missed out on the chance to become one of the signatories of the 'Loyal Address to His Majesty' from the people of Frome. He had sent two letters to fellow magistrate Rev Sainsbury asking that his name be attached but that gentleman had declined, on the grounds of his 'determination not to enter any other name than his own'. This should have come as no surprise. A public meeting had been held in Frome on 2 December to organise the address and alongside Sainsbury the organisers included Thomas Bunn, James Wickham and George Kingdon, along with more of his old adversaries. There was a heated discussion as to the form of the address with many suggested amendments. A vote was taken which supported the unamended version by 201 votes to 75. Not everyone was happy. One of Somerset's two MPs, Sir Thomas Buckler Lethbridge, refused to accompany Sir Charles Bampfylde when he presented it to the King on the grounds that they believed the Queen's guilt to be 'fully borne out by the evidence and is sorry that the bill should have been withdrawn.' The text of the Frome Address does not seem to have survived, though there are examples of many others from various parts of the country.

Exclusion from the official proclamation gave Champneys an opportunity to write one of his own and express his undying loyalty in the most convoluted and tortured prose in an address to *The Taunton Courier* newspaper. It is enough for our proposes to reprint his covering letter sent from 2, West Place, West Square, Newington, London and dated 9 December 1820, (still within the confines of the King's Bench),

> Sir, I have the honour to enclose you the copy of an address that I have considered it is necessary to publish for my neighbours in Froome and its vicinity. As my family have been resident the 25 generations at Orchardleigh Park near Froome – as I have acted as a magistrate in that county, and Wiltshire for upwards of 20 years, and am only temporarily, (I trust) absent, I hope my appeal will not be deemed intrusive. Should you consider it worthy of your notice any extracts from it will greatly oblige me,
>
> I have to apologise for intruding upon you and am sir your faithful humble servant
>
> Thomas Champneys

Large sectors of the population celebrated the end of the matter but Caroline was excluded from the coronation and died in the summer of the following year. In July 1821 Thomas Champneys Esq became Sir Thomas Champneys, baronet, following the death of his father on the 2nd of that month at his estate in Exton, Hampshire at the age of 75.

On Tuesday 25 September 1821 Sir Thomas, was released from the King's Bench and appeared in person at the Union Hall Police Court for the second day of the trial of a 21-year-old man named Henry Palmer accused of having 'made away with some bills of exchange' belonging to him. Champneys' case was that Palmer had called upon him on Sunday

28 July 1820 claiming to be a bill broker who had heard that Champneys was in urgent need of a sum of money. This Palmer claimed he was able to get for him as he had been in business on the Royal Exchange for some years. Champneys gave him bills of exchange totalling £2,000 drawn by George Higgins his trusted servant. Instead of selling these bills at a discount to raise the immediate cash that Champneys needed, various investments were made – allegedly on the plaintiff's behalf. These included the purchase of a valuable canteen of cutlery supposed to have belonged to Napoleon Bonaparte, which Palmer had obtained for £500 and an amazing fifty dozen bottles of claret. The canteen it was claimed was worth £800. Sir Thomas and Palmer argued over it, with Champneys saying that he didn't want an investment, he wanted cash as he had what he called 'a matter of great consequence' in the Court of Chancery and had to have 100 guineas immediately.

Palmer eventually handed over that amount which is the only money that Sir Thomas ever received from the deal, although Palmer claimed that he had also handed over £300 worth of watches and the further sum of £150 which was vehemently denied. There were also promises of a gold snuffbox worth 150 guineas and a racehorse worth 100 guineas. Initially Palmer had promised to turn the bills into cash within 7 to 10 days but no money had been forthcoming, and when the money has still not arrived by September Sir Thomas wrote to Palmer stating,

> I know but one principle for an honest man to act to – do as you would be done by, – only change places, if you had given me security for £2000 as I have giving you and received nothing in return what would you say? All I now ask is the return of my securities.

In the course of the court's examination Sir Thomas stated that his property had recently been valued at £350,000 but that he had been greatly embarrassed in financial circumstances for the last 30 years, during which time he had been raising money by annuities, mortgages on his revisionary interest in his father's estate, and by negotiating bills of exchange. He also admitted that he had been driven to such lengths as purchasing timber, velvet, silks etc on credit and reselling them at great loss to raise urgent cash. He said that during this time he had been the victim of about 40 swindling moneylenders and that he had a list of the scoundrels who had been pecking at him and endeavouring to obtain his securities, tending to his utter ruin. He admitted that he had raised money by these means to the amount of some £200,000. He was greatly embarrassed by his circumstances but had considerable expectations upon the death of his father, at that time still living. The magistrate found that there was a case to answer and remanded Palmer to the next Assizes on bail of £2,000. As the court was waiting for Palmer's sureties to be taken they received a note saying that Palmer had been arrested for a similar offence against a Mr Lowndes. Nonetheless, bail was granted and even reduced to two sureties of £125 pounds each.

The case proper opened at the Surrey Assizes in Kingston on Monday April 1st 1822. This time there was another defendant alongside 25-year-old Palmer, who was described as an 'advertising moneylender'; Thomas Joshua Park, proprietor of the Clarendon Hotel, Bond Street who, it was alleged, had been part of the conspiracy to obtain Sir Thomas's money. The defendants denied that was any conspiracy and that Champneys was a man 'hackneyed in the ways of the world' who could not complain of having been deceived and that no fraud had been committed upon him, his bills were complete wastepaper, they claimed, and he and his servant Higgins were themselves conspirators in drawing and accepting bills to deceive the world, and the defendants were the sufferers who had been 'deluded out of the money by the designing ingenuity of the prosecutor'.

Despite their protestations the whole affair was exposed as being a conspiracy from the start with several other victims, and after a short deliberation the defendants were found guilty. During sentencing on 11 June, Justice Bayley described Sir Thomas as a weak man, 'the weakest of dupes' who had been preyed upon by the defendants, but noted that all the bills had been returned so that Sir Thomas was no longer liable for them. This induced the court not to inflict a fine which is what they would have done under normal circumstances. The judge deeply regretted that he should have this office to perform towards men who appeared to have born a reputable character until this time. The court sentenced them both to four months imprisonment in the Coldbath Fields House of Correction.

In the normal course of events that would have been the end of the matter, but a small diversion from the main story is worthwhile. A full 10 years later Henry Palmer was in the dock once more, this time at the Middlesex Sessions charged with an almost identical set of offences. In

July 1833 an advertisement appeared in a morning newspaper supposedly by a retired businessman who had a sum of £20,000 that he was prepared to lend at an interest rate of 4.5%. The offer was taken up by the eldest son of Sir J Astley the MP for Wiltshire, Francis Dugdale Astley, who was in dire need of £5,000 to pay some gambling debts. A deal was struck with a solicitor and professional fraudster named John Minter Hart whereby ten bills of exchange valued at £500 each were given by Astley to Hart, with the latter promising to go and obtain the money. No money turned up. Astley complained and was basically told that unless he kept quiet his father would be informed of the loan and its purpose – but worse still, so would his father-in-law Sir Thomas Lethbridge, from whom was hoping one day to obtain his fortune. A very similar set of circumstances to those of a decade before.

Astley went to London to look for Hart and after a good deal of investigation Palmer was traced, arrested and charged with conspiring with Hart and several others to steal and sell on the notes. He appeared in the dock described as a fashionably dressed man of gentlemanly manners who resided at Hertford Street, Mayfair and warrants were issued for the arrest of the co-conspirators. The trial took place at the Middlesex Sessions with Palmer alone in the dock and after a lengthy trial he was convicted by the jury within five minutes. When it was time for sentence the prosecution brought up the subject of his previous convictions and the case involving Sir Thomas was mentioned with that previous victim actually appearing in court, where to everyone's amazement he failed to recognise the prisoner, 'after earnestly surveying him for some time' and left the building! Unfortunately for Palmer the officer who had taken him down to Kingston ten years before was on hand and able to make a definite identification. Palmer was sentenced to be transported for 14 years, upon which he collapsed in the dock and had to be carried to the cells and thence to Newgate.

Once again the matter seemed to have ended but there were more twists to come. At the end of October John Minter Hart was finally traced and arrested. He stood in the dock described as 'a remarkably fine and handsome man of about 35 years of age, most respectably dressed and exhibiting the greatest composure and firmness of mind'. He was remanded in custody for a week but before his trial could get underway he applied for the court to be changed on the grounds that Benjamin Rotch, the chairman of the quarter sessions, was a close friend of Sir Thomas Lethbridge, father-in-law of the victim, and that he had done all he could to prejudice the minds of the jury against the defendant, including supplying them with copies of a satirical magazine which contained lots of false information about him. On this basis the defence asked that the case be moved to the Old Bailey and this was agreed with the trial listed to begin in early December 1833. Or that was the plan. The defence argued successfully that the 'pieces of paper' termed bills of exchange were worthless in themselves and that they did not come under the terms of the act, meaning that no felony had been committed. Unbelievably Hart was discharged – only to be rearrested on a separate, lesser charge as he left the court. Even then his luck held. The defence had noticed that the offence was alleged to have been committed in the parish of Marylebone but on the indictment instead of the word 'Middlesex' it said 'City of London' and was therefore invalid. After a short discussion the judges agreed, the case was dismissed, and Hart was released. The upshot of this, of course, was that if no crime had been committed and the conspiracy charge was invalid then the conviction of Palmer must also be unsound. He was eventually granted a free pardon and released from Newgate on 24 December.

Such good luck could not last forever and Hart was soon rearrested on charges of forgery, which this time led to a conviction and on 16 December 1836 he was sentenced at the Old Bailey to be transported for life to Van Diemen's Land. He set sail on a ship called the *Mangles* on the 18 March 1837 and died there not long after.[1] The fate of Henry Palmer is unknown.

~~~

IT SEEMS THAT for Sir Thomas as soon as one court door closed another swung open – or two in this case. While he was at Kingston for the Palmer trial on Tuesday 2 April 1822 his second case against Messiter for bribing witnesses, the basis of the 1820 slander trial, was called on at Taunton before Justice Burrough for 8am on Thursday 4th, and at a distance of about 140 miles. Sir Thomas would not be able to get there in time for the start of proceedings and so he sent a note to the court saying that he and his attorney Harrison would not be able to appear until
~~~

the afternoon.[2] Despite the defence offering to admit what it could of the prosecution case to save time, Burrough said that he would not wait any longer and retired. Sir Thomas eventually arrived at 3.00pm having taken the express coach from Kingston but was too late and the Messiter case was postponed until the assizes in August.

Champneys' debts showed no signs of going away and his run of bad luck no sign of improving. Far from it. From 26 May 1822 at the Guildhall he was involved in a number of linked court appearances which dragged on in various forms until August 1823. The Guildhall case was brought by a Mr Pye who was claiming £500 on a bill of exchange which he maintained had not been honoured. Champneys lost and had £510 interest added to his debt.

Confinement within the Rules, whilst giving a large amount of personal freedom, plunged Champneys into a den of con men, fraudsters and loan sharks who specialised in preying on their unfortunate fellow inhabitants by seeking out those recently sentenced and desperate for some way out of their predicament. During his stay there during June 1820 he had been lodging in a house with a fellow bankrupt named Edward McGrath who had once been an army paymaster, and the two became friends, or so Sir Thomas thought. When he heard about Champneys' difficulties, he suggested a way in which he could raise some cash through a wealthy coachmaker named Maberly, involving an exchange of acceptances which McGrath claimed were as 'good as the Bank of England'. During December an exchange took place in the sum of £5,000, Maberly giving his acceptances and receiving those of Champneys in return. McGrath omitted to include the fact that Maberly was himself a bankrupt and no stranger to the courts. The defence claimed that Champneys had been dealing in bills all his life and was unlikely to have been taken in so easily, presumably the defence team had not had dealings with Sir Thomas before.

The prosecution called a number of character witnesses against Champneys to say that his evidence could not be trusted, and amongst them was a Mr Noah Edward Lewis of 3 Melina Place, Westminster Road who had himself been imprisoned under the King's Bench Rules. Lewis, an accountant, who had also been an army paymaster, had been appointed to the 8th Royal Veteran Battalion in 1805, during which time he had stood trial and been acquitted of a £5,000 fraud. In May1814 Lewis had been convicted of embezzling £2,280 of the battalion's money and dismissed from the service.[3] Lewis claimed to have known Champneys for three years and deposed that his word could not be trusted.

Presumably Lewis was another of the con men who frequented the area – Sir Thomas must have drawn them like moths to a flame. He never received the promised money and his bills were sold on to others, who in turn took him to court and, as he was unable to prove his good faith and show that he had been duped, he lost the case in May 1822 with damages of over £2000 awarded against him. Doubtless he shrugged, bowed to the judge and added this amount to all his other debts.

When he wasn't in jail or trying to avoid it, he was involved in a variety of other legal cases. One brought before the court during June of 1822 was against a Richard Panford who was a tenant at Orchardleigh. While Champneys was confined to London he thought he could get away with not paying his rent but upon Champneys showing proof of ownership he lost the case and was ordered to hand over £2,000.

In July of 1822 there was the very odd case of Thomas Oddy, a former butler at Orchardleigh who was charged with stealing a pistol. According to the evidence given at Bridgwater a man named George King was given the pistol as a present by Oddy in March 1820. In September 1822 King noticed some placards around the estate relating to 'dilapidations at Orchardleigh and family portraits'. The meaning of this is unclear but probably relates to items either stolen or seized by bailiffs while Champneys was away and which he was hoping to recover. Whatever the cause King took it into his head that Oddy had stolen the pistol that he had given to him. It seems an odd way to show gratitude for a present and the pair had undoubtedly fallen out on some other matter. In a very confused report it seems that King had convinced Champneys that the pistol had been stolen from him and it was Champneys that brought the prosecution. When King's name was called to give evidence, he was not to be found, but there were a number of people who claimed that he was an unreliable person who had served time in prison and the case was dismissed.

[1] Newgate Calendar Vol 2 1836
[2] Messiter 1822 p. 5
[3] Military Register 1814-05-25

11
MESSITER AND RELEASE

On 14 August 1822 the case against Messiter for 'Endeavouring to persuade 4 persons to falsely swear that Sir Thomas Champneys had attempted to commit ------etc', finally began at Wells before Justice Richardson. Why it had taken Champneys two years to bring the action is not known but it should be remembered that he was still confined to London for debt and would be until the following September, presumably it was difficult to organise the case and witnesses under those restrictions. The basic contention was that Messiter had been afraid of losing his forthcoming trial for slander and had gone around town trying to get people to appear in court on his behalf to swear that they had heard the same rumours and believe them to be true. The prosecution opened by stating that Sir Thomas was 'a gentleman whose life, in many portions of it, has been marked by misfortune'.

Three witnesses were called by Mr Serjeant Pell for the prosecution,

The first was James Keington a carpenter and joiner from Rode who had worked at Orchardleigh some years ago and who claimed to have known Messiter for about seven or eight years. He gave evidence that Messiter had visited his shop on 8 May 1820 and had offered to overlook a £15 debt if he would give evidence that he knew something of a 'dirty report' about Champneys and that Champneys had 'made attempts upon him'. Messiter also promised that he would 'make a gentleman of me all the days of my life' but Keington refused, saying that he didn't know anything about it and declared that he knew nothing against Sir Thomas personally but did add that 'he had heard reports'. He was threatened with being subpoenaed to appear in court and with imprisonment. Messiter did not deny that the meeting took place but claimed that he was merely seeking information and offered no threats or inducements. Keington, claimed Messiter, had asked for £20 to give evidence but the offer was rejected; an accusation that was strongly denied by the witness.

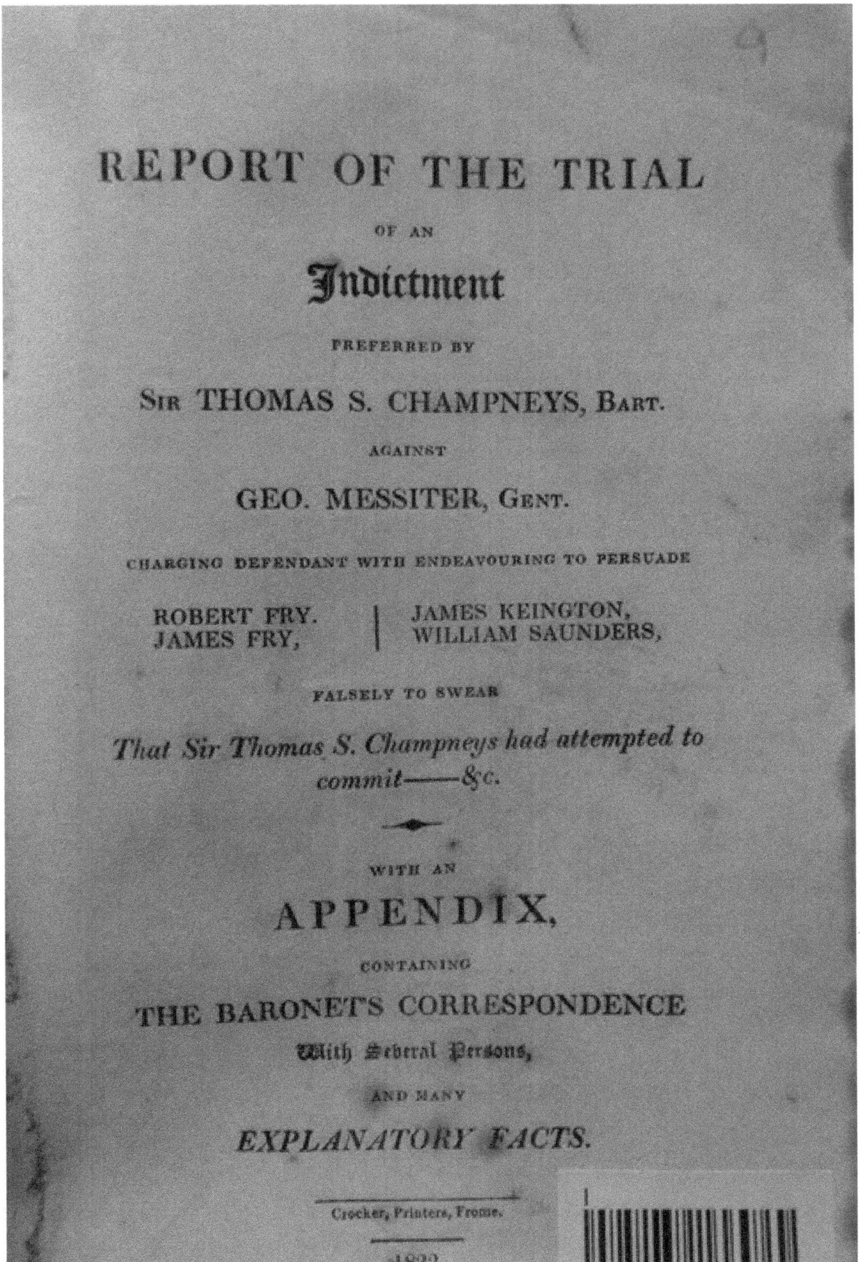

REPORT OF THE TRIAL

OF AN

Indictment

PREFERRED BY

SIR THOMAS S. CHAMPNEYS, BART.

AGAINST

GEO. MESSITER, GENT.

CHARGING DEFENDANT WITH ENDEAVOURING TO PERSUADE

ROBERT FRY.
JAMES FRY,
JAMES KEINGTON,
WILLIAM SAUNDERS,

FALSELY TO SWEAR

That Sir Thomas S. Champneys had attempted to commit——&c.

WITH AN

APPENDIX,

CONTAINING

THE BARONET'S CORRESPONDENCE

With Several Persons,

AND MANY

EXPLANATORY FACTS.

Crocker, Printers, Frome.

1822.

The title page of the trial transcript published by Messiter

The next witness was Robert Fry, the 'agent' who had given evidence in the previous trial. He was living in London in 1820 when Messiter called and asked to see Fry's son William about the allegations but was told that he was in the country. His other son James Fry, a wool spinner of Lullington, was at this time serving a sentence of two years in prison having been sentenced at the Salisbury Assizes for the theft of 60 yards of cloth valued at £40. It seems that he was also engaged in the prison as a schoolmaster. James was called but not examined as the defence objected that the court could not allow the evidence of a convicted felon, whether elevated to prison schoolmaster or not, and so it is not known what evidence was expected of him other a repetition of his evidence in the slander trial. Robert Fry is possibly the clothier of Lullington who had attempted to found a bank next to his mill but had become bankrupt in 1808 and was sentenced to deportation but later pardoned. Robert Fry was also involved with a court case against George Messiter's banker father Nathaniel involving the ownership of some machinery worth £500 which Messiter had seized from Fry to settle a debt of £500 dating back to 1815. Messiter lost the action and had £376 in damages awarded against him. As can be seen there was no love lost between the two parties.

The final witness was William Saunders, now a butcher of Tamworth Street, Lichfield, but at one time employed as gamekeeper for many years by Champneys 10 to 12 years before. Messiter had travelled all the way to Lichfield to question Saunders during June 1820, saying that he heard from William Corner that he, Saunders, could prove Champneys to be a sodomite who had made attempts on a man named Cuzner. Saunders denied ever having heard of 'such a name as Cuzner'.

It will be remembered that Corner was also a former gamekeeper on Champneys' estates and the owner of the greyhound dog shot on Champneys orders many years before.[1] Saunders denied that he had heard any genuine reports about Mr Champneys and Cuzner and replied that,' I told him I had, but among the lower order of the people and I did not believe anything of it. Messiter insisted that I must come to the Assizes in Wells to tell the court what I had heard and he offered me money to do so'.[2] Messiter admitted in his note to the trial report [3] that Saunders had offered to contact another witness and that he had offered to pay for Saunders' bed, board and time if he would go and find him. A letter to this effect was produced in court so that he could hardly deny it. Saunders said that he had attended court on the previous occasion but was not called to give evidence.

In his closing speech Gaselee for Messiter claimed that Champneys' team had asked the judge if evidence as to Champneys' character could be brought in and were assured that it could not. The present trial was purely vindictive, stated Gaselee, and brought about because Champneys did not think that Messiter had received sufficient punishment at the previous trial.

Mr Justice Richardson summed up, the jury retired to consider their verdict and after two hours they returned with a verdict of GUILTY.

Messiter immediately put in an appeal and the King's Bench sitting in Westminster set the verdict aside until the following November, after which the case was once more postponed but nothing further seems to have been reported on the matter, and either it just petered out or Messiter won on appeal, as he was still listed as an attorney in the Frome census of 1841 despite his serious convictions.

At the conclusion of the trial in August Messiter had applied for his costs against Champneys for his wasted time at Taunton some months before when the case had to be abandoned due to Champneys non-appearance, and he was awarded £156 1s 4d against Champneys. To obtain this sum Messiter had to serve papers on Sir Thomas in person and when he attempted to do this on the steps of the court Champneys refused to accept them calling him an 'impertinent puppy' for addressing him, at which Messiter called the baronet *A BEAST!*

There are no reports of an actual physical assault but Champneys declared his intention to have him arrested, though it seems that nothing came of this. In all probability nothing came of either case because Sir Thomas's problems became much worse and he was in Ilchester jail from 26 July 1823 – but that is for a later chapter. In the meantime he was at last freed from confinement in London and on his way home.

Despite all the mudslinging, rumours and debts, it seems that he was genuinely loved by a large number of the local population. Maybe his easy way with money and roguish reputation struck a chord with the man in the street; maybe it was his fairness as a magistrate. Whatever the reason both extremes of the social spectrum often united against the middlemen or professional class in the town.

On Monday 5 September 1822 he returned to Orchardleigh after an absence of over two years within the Rules of the King's Bench. J O Lewis says that Lady Champneys provided a large part of her personal fortune to have him released, and quite possibly there was some money from his father's estate following his death the previous summer. Contemporary press reports state that a body of his friends, tenants and neighbours marched with him to the house bearing several banners with the mottos 'Welcome Home', 'The Upright Magistrate', 'The Kind Landlord', 'The Poor Man's Friend', 'The Oppressor's Scourge,' 'Liberty, Loyalty, Integrity, Truth', and so on. He was accompanied by two bands of music which met him on the road from Trowbridge and proceeded to escort him through Beckington and Frome to the principal entrance of Orchardleigh Park on the Buckland Road. As the cavalcade advanced the multitude increased and extended for almost a mile. In Frome the streets were literally crammed with many wearing their Sunday clothes and as they approached Woolverton they were accompanied by a band of 14 musicians in a carriage drawn by six horses followed by a car containing six beautiful young women dressed in white with blue favours and carrying baskets of flowers to strew the road. Then followed the Honourable Baronet's carriage drawn by eight young men in appropriate dress with short smock frocks, white straw hats and favours after which came 20 horsemen with banners inscribed 'Champneys For Ever!' The procession had increased with every village it passed during a total of 10 miles, and during its progress Sir Thomas frequently addressed the populace with singular energy in effective and appropriate language which at times pointedly touched upon the cause of his absence from home.

As one newspaper reported, 'Upon entering Orchardleigh, the park was thronged with pedestrians, equestrians, and accompanied by a discharge of maroons and rockets. Refreshments were provided for the people and the health of Sir Thomas was drank with enthusiasm. At 6 o'clock a party of the principal tenants etc numbering about 50 dined at Woolverton where Sir Thomas presided. In the evening there was an immense bonfire, made of 600 faggots with a high pole in the centre upon which was roasted legs of mutton with unlimited beer and a grand display of fireworks. It should be noted that not one single accident occurred during the whole day.' History is of course silent as to who organised and paid for this magnificent display...

On 30 September he was treated to a dinner at the George Hotel for over 100 people to celebrate his return by the 'gentlemen and tradesmen of Frome'. Tickets were one guinea each and Sir Thomas gave a speech of great length that was much applauded.

In the same month he had the remains of his father removed from the church at Exton, where they had been deposited during his absence, and reinterred in the family vault at the church of St Mary Orchardleigh.[4]

[1] Messiter p 36
[2] Messiter p 34
[3] Messiter p 37
[4] Morning Post 1822-10-22

12
JAMAICA, PRISON AND LITIGATION 1822-1827

IN 1822, AFTER the death of Sir Thomas in July 1821, Thomas Swymmer inherited lands in Saint Thomas in the East district on the Nutt's River in Jamaica which had passed down through his mother's family the Swymmers. The origins of the Champneys connection to the sugar plantations can be traced back to 1739 when, on 25 September, Richard Champneys aged 43 married his second wife Jane Langley Swymmer of Mold, Flintshire (1722-1752) at the age of 23. She was eventually the sole heiress[1] of her brother Anthony Langley Swymmer (1725-1760)[2] and inherited the plantations and large amounts of land on the island.[3] Anthony Swymmer was born on the south-east coast of Jamaica where the family had been early colonists, starting with his grandfather Anthony Swymmer who died in 1688. The family were merchants from Bristol and prominent in the municipal life of that town in the 17th and 18th centuries. He attended Winchester College and Peterhouse Cambridge and was returned as Tory MP for Southampton in 1747 and remained so until his death 1760. He married Arabella Astley daughter of Sir John Astley, of Patshull, Staffordshire in 1748, and they lived at Longwood House in Southampton when not in Jamaica; the family also had extensive estates in Mold, Flintshire.

Swymmer died childless on 4 January 1760 in Jamaica aged 34 and in his will he outlined his West Indian holdings as, Nutt's River of around 2,036 acres; Clarke's River, also in St Thomas-in-the-East of 1,120 acres; a parcel of 332 acres of land bought from Richard Risby adjoining Nutt's River; 4,000 acres at Milk River in Vere called Swymmer's Land or Milk River Land; a parcel of about 1,100 acres of land in St George's; and land in Spanish Town near the beef market. Upon his death all this passed to Richard Champneys through his wife Jane.

When Richard Champneys died in 1760 his properties were found to be subject to annuities totalling £1,560 per annum to friends and family with a mortgage of £4,000, as well as an additional security for a further £4,000 secured on the Mold estate, to Henry Swymmer of Bristol. He left the estate thus encumbered, with additional legacies of £5,000 to his niece Sarah Champneys.[4] The whole sum of his debts was far more than the estate could bear and when Richard died he left the estates and all the debts in trust to his son Thomas.

In 1775 Sir Thomas now in his early 30s went to live in Jamaica for a period leaving his wife and children in England and took up various government and legal positions. Records show that during the period 1782-84 he was an assistant judge of the Common Pleas and one of the superintendents of forts on the Windward side from 1784-90.[5] Despite his efforts to make the investments pay, by the mid 1780s the revenues from his plantations were in decline due to bad weather conditions and competition from the other islands. According to an inventory of slaves taken on 26 June 1820 on the estate in the parish of St Thomas their lands contained 263 African and mixed-race slaves. The slave trade was officially abolished in 1808 but the keeping of slaves remained legal until 1833.

In 1822 the court of the King's Bench heard the case of Champneys v John and Philip Vaughan, Bristol merchants, in which Thomas Swymmer sought to recover the produce of his estates in Jamaica for the previous year to the value of around £10,000. The defendants had received the goods but refused to deliver them under what they believed to be the terms of a trust on the orders of Richard Henry Cox, uncle to Thomas Swymmer who had a large measure of control over his expenditure at home and abroad. The Vaughans had been handling the proceeds of the plantations for around 60 years and were quite blameless in the affair to which they offered no defence. The court found that the terms of the trust had died with Sir Thomas and his son was awarded the £10,000 and a receiver was appointed to sort the affair out. This ruling was appealed by Cox but again rejected by the court.

In June 1824 Champneys sold some of the estates to David Wakefield, a barrister of Middlesex, and William Davis Bayly also a barrister born in Frome in 1796 and who lived at Garston Lodge but practiced at the Inner Temple – the same person who had been involved

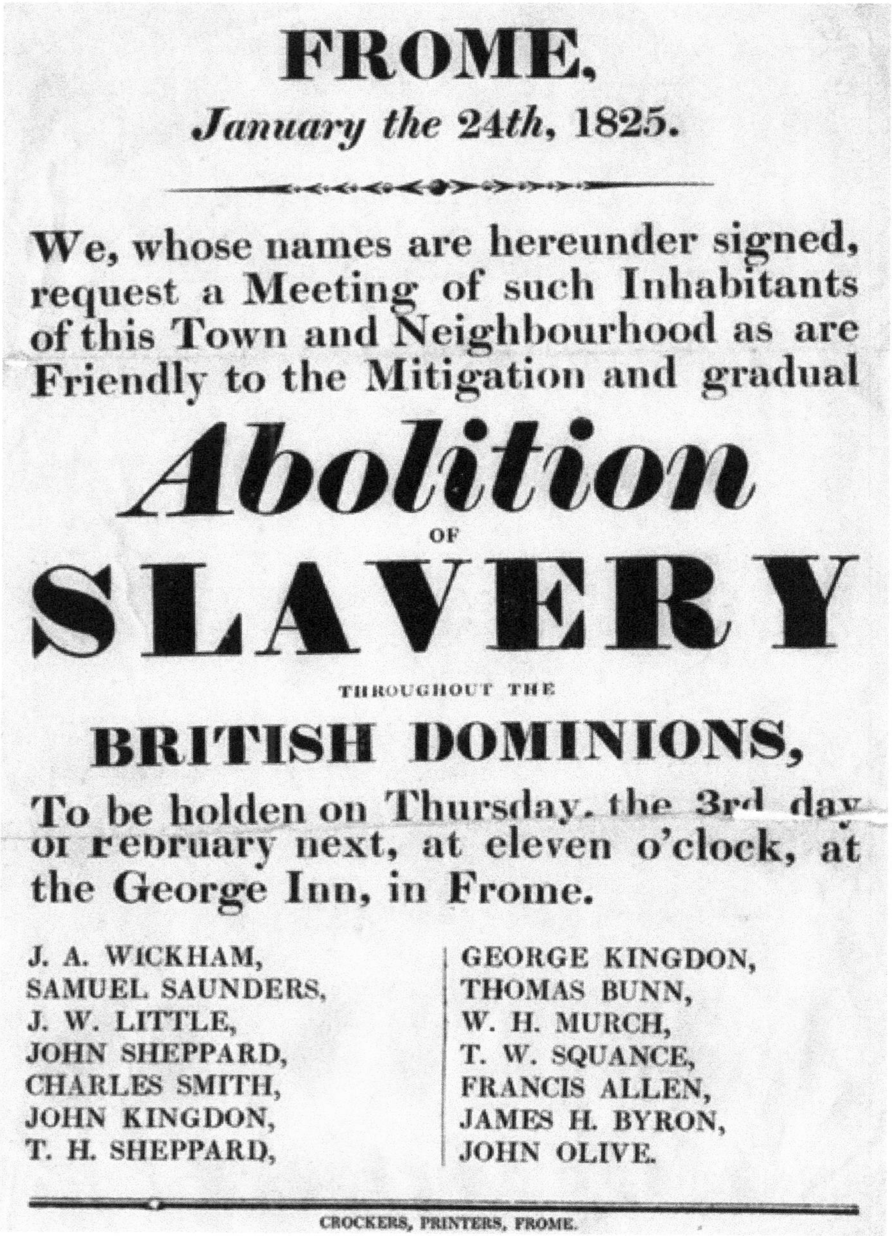

FROME,

January the 24th, 1825.

We, whose names are hereunder signed, request a Meeting of such Inhabitants of this Town and Neighbourhood as are Friendly to the Mitigation and gradual

Abolition

OF

SLAVERY

THROUGHOUT THE

BRITISH DOMINIONS,

To be holden on Thursday, the 3rd day of February next, at eleven o'clock, at the George Inn, in Frome.

J. A. WICKHAM,
SAMUEL SAUNDERS,
J. W. LITTLE,
JOHN SHEPPARD,
CHARLES SMITH,
JOHN KINGDON,
T. H. SHEPPARD,
GEORGE KINGDON,
THOMAS BUNN,
W. H. MURCH,
T. W. SQUANCE,
FRANCIS ALLEN,
JAMES H. BYRON,
JOHN OLIVE.

CROCKERS, PRINTERS, FROME.

An anti-slavery poster of 1825 signed by many of Thomas Swymmer's adversaries with him in efforts to alleviate the poor in Frome many years before, as we have seen.[6] Between them and a George Tuson they acquired 1,167 acres of the Nutts River Plantation along with a dwelling house, outhouses, windmill, boiling house, curing house, hill house, and all other buildings. Also included were 1,120 acres with its slave workforce, about 2,348 acres in total.

Richard Henry Cox stepped in as Sir Thomas Champneys' affairs deteriorated, mortgaging his remaining manors of Orchardleigh and Frome Selwood, along with the Nutt's River sugar plantation. Richard Cox foreclosed on Champneys' eventual bankruptcy, and Cox and Co. held the lands until 1854.

~~~

IN 1823 THE whole Orchardleigh estate was placed in Chancery and Champneys was imprisoned in Ilchester jail on 26 July at the age of 54, less than a year after his triumphant return from London.[7] No details of the circumstances of his arrest have been traced except that he was delivered to the jail by Constable Ivey on that date. During the eighteenth and nineteenth centuries around 10,000 people were imprisoned for debt each year. A prison term did not alleviate a person's debt and an inmate was typically required to repay the creditor in full before being released. The prisons varied in the amount of freedom they allowed the debtor and Ilchester was a far cry from his time within the King's Bench Rules but, with a little money, he could pay for some privileges; however, insolvent debtors could be kept in prison indefinitely if their creditors so wished.

The Ilchester jail and house of correction was situated at Northover, on the north bank of the River Ivel, by 1615 and was extended by the addition of 26 cells in 1789. By 1808 the prison had a quadrangular plan, with buildings ranged around courtyards. Dayrooms were located on the ground floor with sleeping cells on the floors above. Lying south of the men's ward were the debtor's apartments, a stable and cow house and a carpenter's shop and conversation room. On the west side of the prison was an L-plan female prison. By 1821 a number of additions had been made. A detached building north of the gaoler's house, containing a wash house and a bakehouse on the ground floor and a laundry on the
~~~

first floor, had been erected by 1810. The courtyards had been subdivided and additions had been made to the debtors' section. The prison closed in March 1843.

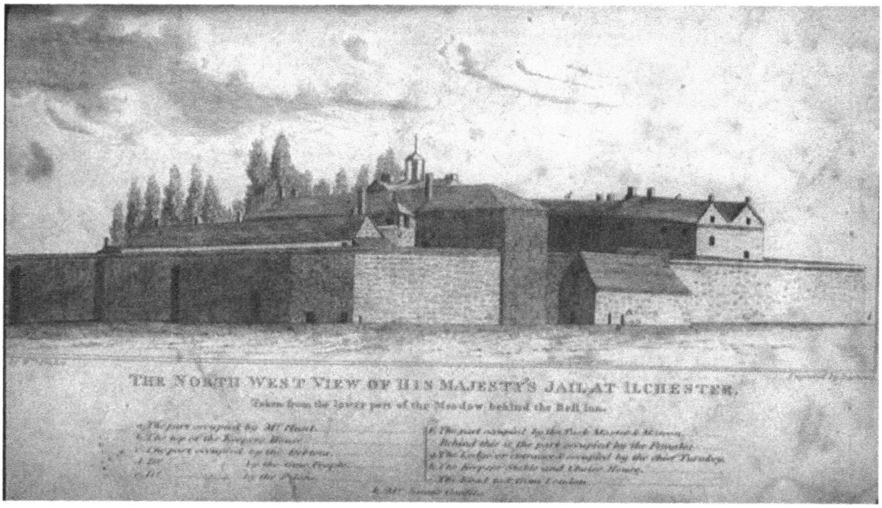

Ilchester Jail

One of his many problems concerned a pair of money lenders named Howard and Gibbs, operating as the Star Life Annuity Office in London. The case dates back to 1818 when, in desperation, Champneys borrowed £33,000 from the company – or thought that he had. This seems to have been an attempt to consolidate all his regular outgoings into one loan. and resulted in yet another long-running case. The pair demanded 12% interest on the advance and 9% for procuring the money, and it seems that Star Life took at least some of the interest off the total sum in advance and held on to most of the rest to settle other of his annuities without his consent. Sir Thomas took the company to court, won his case and the loan at a repayable and legal rate of 5%. The case set a legal precedent in which it was stated that the whole of the agreed sum must be paid to the borrower in such cases with no deductions.

Despite this large sum not all the creditors could be satisfied and he was taken to court once more, in the case of Groom and Others. Eventually an agreement was reached whereby the claims were set aside on condition that Champneys pay the amount of £12,678 by a certain day. The deadline came and went without the money being repaid and at the resulting court appearance in February 1824 he was granted a further period of time, but as he was in jail the chances of the date being met were pretty much non-existent. In the following May yet another extension of a fortnight was granted but proved as fruitless as the others. In that year Champneys estates were valued at around £300,000 and placed in trust for his claimants with a proviso that his personal liberty be guaranteed. The deed of trust which outlined these terms was for some reason not executed and the arrangement failed, which caused him to enter into a contract with Sir Walter Stirling of Stirling Hodsoll and Co, a London banker. The new deal was that all claimants were to be paid off within six months, the sum of £2,000 per annum was to be granted to Sir Thomas and the income from his West Indian estates was to be released. The bank failed in December 1825 and Sir Thomas's unbelievable run of bad luck was set to continue.

Whilst in Ilchester, and presumably between the court cases, he busied himself by making some complaints about the governor, William Erasmus Hardy, who had only taken up the position two years before and now had overall responsibility for 443 inmates. On 7 June 1824 Champneys wrote to one of the visiting magistrates at the jail, a Vincent Stuckey of Langport. In rather tortuous prose he complains that he is being deprived of any proper exercise within the jail and that Governor Hardy is guilty of many infringements of the prison rules, including cruel and inhumane treatment of prisoners and misuse of prison property for his own purposes.[8] He says that he has proof of cruel treatment against 'a man and a woman' but gives no details. A note by Stuckey written on 12 July 1824 on the back of a letter states that Champneys had agreed to postpone charges until his release from jail – probably a wise decision under the circumstances. The matter was further complicated by Champneys' main witness, a turnkey named Davis, having some trouble on his own account.

In April 1826 Davis, who had agreed to act as a witness in support of Champneys' claims, brought a civil case of his own against Hardy claiming damages for malicious prosecution, the facts of which included having him arrested, lodged with felons in his own jail and other cruel treatment. Hardy had charged Davis with having pocketed a sum of money that was to pay for transporting a debtor to court in Taunton, but when the matter came to court no witnesses could be produced and the case was dropped, leading to the malicious prosecution charge. The whole case, claimed Davis, was totally untrue and brought maliciously to discredit the forthcoming Champneys case. However, further investigations had shown that the allegations could quite possibly be true and, in the meantime, Davis had been sacked by the magistrates responsible for his employment, for other misdemeanours, his character blackened and any evidence that he might have brought in Champneys' favour would not have carried much weight. Neither case went any further.

These were not the only complaints against Hardy involving cruelty and ill treatment. He and his son Joseph were charged before a grand jury at Bridgwater in July 1824 with assaulting a Mr Smith from Bath, who was also imprisoned for debt. Some of the allegations were that Smith was kept in irons and shackled to a bed in a dark damp cell for 20 hours and that he was kept in prison for 11 days after his discharge had arrived.

The allegations were made in a newspaper called *John Bull* published and largely written by a fun-loving and rather dissolute eccentric called Theodore Hook. On September 13th Champneys had a long letter published in the *Morning Post*, during which he claims to have, 'made the most minute and particular enquiries into the allegations.... and obtained it to the extent of a full, clear and decided confirmation upon oath of every point with which Mr Smith has charged the jailer. Such testimony extended to no fewer than nine different witnesses. and that, under an experience of 30 years as a county magistrate ...I never met a case more decidedly supported by consistent testimony than the one before us'.

Despite his insistence upon the truth of the allegations the witnesses must have been unwilling to come forward and the case was dismissed, but worse was to follow. The editors of *John Bull* were asked to substantiate the allegations and, when they could not, Hardy sued for libel. The paper pleaded guilty and in a behind the scenes deal, in which both sides seem to have agreed to play the matter down, escaped with an agreed nominal fine of 40 shilling plus costs. Mr Smith's thoughts on the matter are unrecorded.

On 22 May 1826, Frome auctioneers Ryall and Harrold announced that the contents of Orchardleigh House, including furniture, paintings by eminent masters, musical instruments, breakfast dinner and tea services, elegant china, cut glass, plate, bed and table linen and other valuable effects, were to be auctioned on the following Monday and for five days thereafter. The lots were fully described in catalogues available five days prior to the sale at one shilling each and no one was to be admitted without one. In the same month the local papers were reporting that a vein of coal been discovered on the estate, though nothing seems to have come of this. In another bizarre report it was stated that the counterpane which covered the bed of Charles I the night before his execution and which is made of a very rich thick blue satin, embroidered with gold and silver in a deep border, has continued to be used by the family as a christening mantel from the time it came into their possession by marriage when one of the Champneys married the sole heiress of the Chandlers of Camms Hall near Fareham in Hampshire, a family connected with Cromwell. The sword belt of the unfortunate king was also said to be in the house.

~~~

ASIDE FROM CHAMPNEYS' personal problems June 1826 was the time of a general election. This was of course before the great reform act and Somerset returned just two MPs Champneys was still in Ilchester jail and any views he may have had on the outcome remain unknown. However, during the campaign and according to the newspapers, Frome was 'constantly harangued' by a man named Henry Hunt otherwise known as 'Orator' Hunt a well-known political radical. Hunt was a Wiltshire man whose main claim to fame was his involvement in the Peterloo Massacre of 1819 when a meeting of 80,000 people in Manchester in favour of Parliamentary reform was broken up by the local yeomanry, resulting in the deaths of 11 people. Hunt was charged with 'unlawful and seditious assembling for the purpose of expressing discontent' and sentenced to two and a half years in Ilchester jail; he was there from May 1820 until his release in October 1822. Hunt decided to contest the parliamentary seat for Somerset in the election for which voting began in June 1826. He stood no chance of unseating the two long-standing incumbents, William Dickson and Sir Thomas Lethbridge, but used the opportunity to promote the radical cause.
~~~

Although a spellbinding speaker, contemporary reports say that he was in the habit of dealing out abuse and hostility to all persons and classes, but saved a particular venom for attorneys who he called 'land sharks'.

Hunt first appeared in Frome on May 31st. Speaking from a temporary platform in the Market Place he addressed a crowd of about 8,000 people for almost an hour during which time he attacked the sitting MPs as representing no one but the magistrates, attorneys and clergy. He explained the unfairness of the corn laws, cider and salt taxes and the greed of the 'grasping landlords', as he called them, and expressed his determination to stand in the election.

On 17 June his campaigning took him to Frome once more and so successful was he in inflaming the population on this occasion that no attorney could appear in the streets without cries of 'No Land Sharks', and it is reported that the town was in a state of continued riot from the moment that he began to speak. At one time things became so bad that a number of respectable inhabitants were sworn in as special constables in order to preserve the peace. During the afternoon a Mr George Messiter, described as 'a respectable solicitor', who had exchanged some words with Hunt which annoyed the crowd, was approaching his house along Cork Street when he was set upon by a large mob of about 300 who pelted him with stones, surrounding and hooting at him. He managed to escape but three people were arrested and charged with riot. When the case came to court Mr Justice Littledale having heard the prosecution evidence observed that as this riot had only arisen out of an electioneering dispute and was nothing of a character serious enough as to affect the peace of the country he would recommend that the prisoners be allowed to change their pleas to guilty and that the prosecution abandon its case if the prisoners agreed to enter into a recognizance of 50 shillings to keep the peace for 12 months. This was agreed and the prisoners were discharged upon being fined one shilling each.

The poll closed after ten days, and the results were declared at Ilchester after a long slanging match between Hunt and Lethbridge which almost came to blows when the numbers of votes were revealed: Dickinson 1,476, Lethbridge 1,324 and Hunt 257. Dickinson and Lethbridge retained their seats and by far the greatest concentration of support for Hunt was in Frome, which counted 63 votes in his favour followed by Shepton Mallet with 17.[9]

It is interesting to speculate on what Hunt and Champneys would have made of each other. Both had tremendous popular appeal amongst the working population and both were despised by the middle-class; and of course it was only amongst these 'respectable citizens', that there was the right to vote. Unfortunately Hunt left Ilchester jail before Champneys entered it and Champneys was in Ilchester when Hunt was in Frome so it is unlikely that they ever met – they would certainly have had an interesting conversation about the legal profession and Mr Messiter in particular.

While political turmoil raged in his home town Champneys was still in prison and in August 1826 he applied once more to the Commissioner of the Insolvent Debtor's Court at Taunton for his release during which appearance he made 'a most forcible appeal to the court stating that he had suffered so much in mind and body that he was careless of the result'. His release was signed despite strong opposition from one of his creditors, who expressed his determination to keep him incarcerated at any cost. There was a snag however. An incompetent clerk had served some papers on the solicitors rather than the principals in one of the cases, and his release was held up until this could be sorted out. Seeing his distress, 'The Commissioner in a most feeling manner, entreated Sir Thomas not to distress himself and assured him that he saw nothing whatever in the case that could in any way affect or impeach his character'. During the hearing his total worth was estimated at £620,000 and his debts at about £420,000 which the court declared to be the largest ever filed since the court began in 1813.

Champneys remained inside while the paperwork was being attended to, but before his liberation could take effect another problem arose; it emerged that a man named Eley, an attorney from Ilchester, had been missed off the list of creditors and despite diligent inquiries by Mr Bayley, Sir Thomas's solicitor, Mr Eley could not be found, and until he could have his say Sir Thomas had to stay where he was despite denying that he owed him a farthing. On top of this the court was not satisfied with the way in which Bayley had drawn up his affidavit in relation to Eley and so Sir Thomas had to wait while he did it again; he was finally discharged on 20 November 1827 over a year later.

On Monday 3 December, for the time being a free man, Sir Thomas returned home and,

> was greeted in a manner most flattering to his feelings as a magistrate and gentleman, for in passing through Bruton he was saluted with the congratulations of the inhabitants amid a merry peal from the bells of the ancient church; and upon his arriving within four miles of Frome he was met by a large party of tenantry and yeomanry on horseback who escorted him, accompanied by a numerous concourse, to the centre of the town of Frome; where the baronet addressed the great body of the people in the most forcible and poignant language during nearly an hour, after which he re-entered his carriage and was conducted to his mansion at three miles distance amid the heartfelt cheers of the extensive population of that opulent town. Sir Thomas entered upon the late events which have been so much before the public in the fullest manner; and was heard with the most respectful and feeling attention interrupted only by repeated cheers.

It didn't end there, the following Thursday the church bells were rung to celebrate a dinner given by the Yeomanry and tenantry to celebrate his return; the party was described as exceedingly numerous and jovial. Despite all the celebrations, returning home to an empty house and seeing that its contents and collections, which would have taken generations to acquire, had been removed in his absence must have been heart-breaking.

According to John Webb Singer in his newspaper article of 1893 Lady Champneys seemed un-amused by her husband's continued antics and after his release they led separate lives, though both still lived at Orchardleigh. Singer does not give any source for these assertions.[10]

[1] 1803 Pedigree
[2] Gloucestershire, Baptisms, Marriages and Burials, 1538-1813
[3] Legacies of British Slave Ownership, UCL
[4] UCL Anthony Langley Swymmer
[5] *Jamaica Almanac* 1782
[6] Bayly was the author of a pamphlet entitled *The State of the Poor considered; with practical plans for improving their condition in society, and superseding the present system of compulsory assessment.* 1820 Google Books
[7] Ancestry document
[8] SRO Q/AGI/18/1
[9] The History of Parliament website
[10] Reprinted in YB 9 2004

13
1828 THE GEORGE HIGGINS AFFAIR

In January of 1828 St John's Church in Frome was crowded to excess anticipating the appearance of Sir Thomas, who was to receive the church keys as Lord of the Manor and hereditary sexton and place them in the hands of his newly appointed deputy. Champneys was drawn to the church in the sexton's coach drawn by six beautiful grey horses. He usually dressed in a bright blue coat with large brass buttons but on this occasion he wore a red coat. Part of the ceremony was a procession which proceeded from the church to the tower and there he pulled a rope to sound the bell before handing it to the new sexton who did the same, by which act it was announced that the new sexton was now in office.

Champneys had, in recent years, donated almost £500 to buy the site upon which Christchurch and the new burial-ground were built. This induced the inhabitants of Frome to treat him with great respect, causing the church bells to be rung on Sunday and Monday. The new sexton, whose position was described as one of considerable emolument, was George Higgins, Champneys loyal and principal servant, whom he had known since boyhood and who still worked for the estate as well as being a tenant farmer there, and as Sir Thomas put it, 'lay under many obligations to him'.

All seemed to go well for a few months until September of that year when Higgins appeared in court at Mells charged with having violently beaten and ill-treated his master and 'using language thereby putting him in bodily fear'. During the trial Sir Thomas, in typical fashion, embarked upon a speech which lasted three hours outlining his relationship with Higgins. Unfortunately, the details went unreported but it emerged that a previous assault had taken place on 29 August after

Champneys had given Higgins some 'advice relative to his misconduct'. The accused knocked him to the floor and beat him about the head with a stick, and Sir Thomas asked that Higgins be put under sureties to keep the peace – surely a modest request given the severity of the attack, and surely prompting questions about the nature of their relationship. A number of witnesses were called for both sides which occupied over nine hours, and as a result Higgins was bound over in the sum of £100 and required to find two other sureties of £100 each to keep the peace. A co-defendant, John Clarke, a gatekeeper of Orchardleigh, had the charges of threatening language against him dropped at Sir Thomas's request on condition that he drop all connection with Higgins, which he was happy to do.

Unsurprisingly, Sir Thomas now wanted Higgins out of 'his' church and to this end he went around to St John's with his solicitor and two bailiffs. On 7 October the party attended the church, gave Higgins notice to quit, and demanded the keys. Higgins refused and was ordered to be taken into custody, whereupon the two bailiffs placed themselves on each side of him and marched him out of the church through the green and into the churchyard, where they detained him for 10 minutes but were still unable to secure the keys. Higgins went down the pub, where later in the day the two bailiffs produced a warrant and searched him for the keys but couldn't find them, and so one of them stayed with him while the other went off to look for them again without success.

Higgins brought a case against them on the grounds that he had been falsely imprisoned and the court found that the search warrant was illegal, firstly because one could only be issued in the case of a felony or an offence against certain acts of Parliament; secondly because a magistrate could not issue one in his own case; and thirdly, that Sir Thomas Champneys was not to be found on the list of current magistrates in any event! In addition, the conduct of the defendants would not be within the scope of a warrant in any case, as a warrant will not give authority to take a person into custody or detain him. The jury found the defendants guilty and they were fined £5 each. To add insult to injury it seemed likely that, although Sir Thomas had the right to appoint the sexton, he had no right to dismiss him or interfere in his duties, though this had never actually been tested in court.

It seems that Higgins was a hard man to dislodge and he remained a tenant at Orchardleigh's Park Farm until he sold off his dairy stock in February 1830. He died on 30 April 1833 and the office was given to a Mr Hopkins who held it for many years. The vicar had purchased the rights to the sexton's fees by granting him a pension for life – which turned out to be a bad bargain for the vicar as the graveyard was closed by the authorities and few burials took place afterwards. Occasionally Sir Thomas would perform the office of sexton himself, such as when the Bishop visited the church and he would walk before him in some style with a silver badge on the sexton's gown bearing the arms of the Champneys family.

In mid-May 1828 Champneys was sitting as a magistrate when he heard the case of a woman named Sarah Mitchell, the wife of a labouring man in Frome, charged with stealing a quantity of silver-plate from a gentleman's house in Shepton Mallet. As a kindness to the woman, Champneys allowed her to take her seven-month old child into the Bridewell with her. As soon as she was confined to a cell, in a desperate fit of insanity she seized her infant by its legs and dashed its brains out against the bedstead. The wretched woman acknowledged afterwards that she had destroyed another child in the same way and a coroner's inquest returned a verdict of wilful murder against her. It emerged that she was subject to fits of insanity from habitual drinking over many years.

Another of his cases that October involved a man named James Stephen Edgell, a tailor and 'noted informer' who was committed to Shepton jail to await trial for extorting money by threats and false pretences from a baker named Yeoman and others from the town. So greatly was he disliked that it was with some difficulty that Champneys and the peace officers were able to prevent him from being roughly handled by the assembled crowd. The following year he received seven years' transportation for receiving stolen goods and died in Tasmania in 1832.

In December of 1828 Champneys wrote to the home secretary Robert Peel on behalf of an 18-year-old shop worker named William Henry Hulbert, who was confined on the prison hulk *Dolphin* awaiting transportation to Australia for seven years having stolen seven yards of a fabric known as cambric. His original petition does not survive but there are three letters from The Home Office saying that they can see no reason to intervene in the sentence. Hulbert had been convicted at Bristol in April 1827. No further details survive except the prison records which say that he had no prior convictions and was well behaved in prison. He was pardoned in August 1832.

By April of 1829 most of Sir Thomas's rents had been assigned by the courts to pay off various debts, but he still had possession of the main house. But by a judgement in the Court of Chancery brought by The Hon General Frederick St John this too was to be taken from him, even though he had moved out to a lodge in his park and left the mansion in the hands of Lady Champneys and the remaining servants. In the initial judgement he was committed to the Fleet prison for contempt in refusing to give up his house, but Champneys appealed and the Lord Chancellor reversed the order and he was allowed to retain possession of his house.

In April 1831 Sir Thomas Mostyn bart MP died at his house in Park Place, St James aged 55 – unmarried and without issue; the bulk of his estates passed to his eldest sister Lady Charlotte who received £11,000 per year which must have helped their financial problems in some way.

Despite everything that had been through Champneys was not one to shun the limelight and his finest hour was yet to come.

14
THE FROME ELECTION OF 1832

PARLIAMENTARY ELECTIONS WERE to be held for the first time in the new borough of Frome created by the recent Representation of the People Act, and polling was to take place on the 10,11, and 12 December 1832 at the George Inn. Many small landowners, tenant farmers and shopkeepers were able to vote for the first time, and in Frome the total electorate was increased to slightly more than 300 out of a population of 13,000. Thomas Sheppard, a retired London banker who lived on Hampstead Heath in London, was the elder brother by seven years of the woollen mill owner George Sheppard of Fromefield House. He was the first to put himself forward and it was assumed by most that he would stand unopposed. In fact, he had been canvasing for the candidacy since the year before in anticipation of the reform bill going through but within a few weeks Rear Admiral Boyle, brother to the Earl of Cork, who owned large parts of the town and surrounding countryside, expressed an interest in opposing him and announced his intention to stand. Both expressed their support for the principles of reform; in fact, they had appeared together along with many other local dignitaries including Sir Thomas Swymmer Mostyn Champneys at a mass meeting in Frome's Market Place on 15 May.

Speeches were made until a late hour and a petition to King George in support of Earl Grey and the Reform Act is alleged to have received 2,400 signatures within 20 hours.[2] The act passed into law on 7 June. Boyle withdrew towards the end of June and it looked once more like a one-horse race until Sir Thomas agreed to stand and the contest became a straight fight between Sheppard and Champneys. On paper, Champneys was the Tory and Sheppard was for the Whigs; both were men of great power and influence in their mid 60s with a longstanding hatred for each other. Despite all the fine sentiments the election was fought largely on the basis of who could cajole, bribe or otherwise influence the tiny number of electors in their favour. It will be remembered that it was William Sheppard, brother to Thomas Sheppard and long deceased, that had been involved with the dispute over the infantry companies almost 30 years before. The animosity between the two camps ran long and deep. Speeches and meetings by both parties had been in full swing since July but on 28 September a strange piece appeared in the *London Standard*:

> We should be glad to ascertain, from disinterested parties, what is doing and likely to be done at Frome. Was the Mr Thomas Sheppard who had been canvassing that borough among the Tory requisitionists to Mr Lyall to stand for the City of London? If so, men of Frome, be on your guard. There may be wolves in sheep's clothing, and in shepherds also.

On Thursday 18 October Sir Thomas held his first mass rally in the town, accompanied by many of his friends and supporters. The event had been advertised by the handing out of handbills drawn up by the Tories and during the day the Market Place filled with people awaiting his arrival. At 4.00pm he appeared on the balcony of The George Inn accompanied by the church bells which struck up a merry peal. For the following hour and a half he,

> most elaborately explained every point that could be raised in the most fastidious and unsettled mind on the subjects of reform, of Tory principles and Tory candidates. Sir Thomas boldly stated that he considered the supporters of Mr. Lyall (among whom he ranked Mr Thomas Sheppard of Hampstead Heath, his supposed opponent), a combination of as rank and virulent Ultra-Tories as ever emanated from a boroughmongering hotbed, and repeatedly demanded why this candidate for the suffrages of the constituency of Frome did not make his appearance among them and why an individual who canvassed votes upon a principle of reform was to be permitted to rank himself with impunity in the metropolis the most avowed and ultra-enemies of it. The worthy baronet then said in the most emphatic language that he courted not their suffrages: he had come here at their request to Frome – at their request he would retire; on

> having been, as he was, replaced by them in harness, he would touch the collar with the firmness, honesty and zeal, and, if he reached the goal of his ambition they would find him true and faithful to their cause.

After 90 minutes of such eloquent exuberance he was probably in sore need of a drink, (as were most of his audience, it can be imagined – none of whom had the power to vote) and withdrew from the balcony to join a party of his friends in the assembly rooms of the George where they 'partook of a most excellent dinner' prepared by the landlord Mr Hillier. In a great speech he repeated his 'determined resolution to canvas no man for his vote but to enter the House of Commons as an independent member' and went on the explain his views on tithes, the slave trade and other matters of the day – all sadly unrecorded. 'The evening drew to a close at midnight when the Hon Baronet was conducted back to his seat, accompanied by music and the cheers of hundreds of his neighbours.'

The accusation that Sheppard was merely flying a flag of convenience in his support for the Whigs could not be left unchallenged and at the end of October he adopted the tactic that politicians know best – he wriggled. He issued a statement through his agent Harry Miller a solicitor of Welshmill House with an office in Cheap Street, saying that he had indeed, a short time before, attached his signature to support the candidature of Mr George Lyall as Tory candidate for The City of London as be believed him to be a highly gifted commercial man of well-known liberal principles and especially informed on foreign commerce and an honest believer in reform. However, now that Lyall, had publicly declared that, 'to a certain extent he had been a reformer before the bill was proposed but had viewed the measure with distrust fearing it would disturb the harmony existing between different departments of the state', he could see his error of judgment and realised that he had supported that gentleman under a mistaken opinion as to his political sentiments. Sheppard professed himself to be no reactionary Tory but in favour of 'the undelayed extinction of Negro Slavery throughout the British Dominions', and firm supporter of the Whig leader Charles James Fox. He was a believer in the extensive reform of the Church Establishment, the abolition of the tithing system and in favour of compulsory rates and contributions.

The stage was set.

~~~

It is something of a truism that history is written by the victors, and it is certainly true of the events of December 1832. Things started well with much celebration and excitement, a whole ox was roasted at Pilly (Willow) Vale and a massive bonfire built in the Market Place where the Boyle fountain now stands. It was said to have been as high as a house and upon it was placed a huge coffin to represent the end of the old electoral system. The Market Place was crowded with people, flags and bands of music. Local solicitor Thomas Bunn describes his arrival in the Market Place with Sheppard, as the election campaign began,

> I was to nominate one of the candidates. I entered the town with him in a barouche and four with a long procession of well-dressed men, flags and a band of musicians. I was surprised at the Market Place to see a rank of Horsemen in hostile array. The drivers hesitated. I ordered them to force their way through. The flag was torn in pieces and the bearer knocked down. The candidate and his friends ascended the hustings, except myself, and had literally their coats torn to atoms. I drove forward and escaped. All this was instigated by the opposing candidate, a well-known character with whom no gentleman would associate. Our excellent magistrates were at last obliged to shoot some of the mob. I voted against a relation at the county election because his father was a slave holder. I voted for a relation at the borough election because his opponent was a degraded person and it would have been a disgrace to the inhabitants of the town to send such a person to represent them in Parliament.[1]

~~~

The normally accepted view of what happened during the election itself was the subject of a long report issued by Thomas Sheppard and his supporters, the following is their version of events:

> **The Narrative of the Frome Riot.**[3]
> We, the undersigned, declare that we have investigated the facts stated in the following narrative, and that we believe it to be true.

The nomination of candidates for representing the new Borough of Frome was held on Monday the 10th of December. About nine o'clock in the Morning about forty men on foot, bearing Mr Sheppard's favours; and without weapons of any sort, came to Cork Street; and stood quietly near, but not on the steps of the hustings, to protect the approach to them.

Sir Thomas S M Champneys, Bart. arrived at half-past ten, accompanied by many hundred men and boys, many of them armed with bludgeons and cudgels; most of them were on foot, but they were attended by men on horseback. A great number of them wore *white* ribbons, white sashes, or cards inscribed with Sir Thomas Champneys' name; many of them appeared not to be men of Frome; some of their bludgeons and cudgels were loaded with lead.

Some of this party immediately assailed Mr T Sheppard's men, and drove them away from the hustings. The men wearing white colours, then took possession of the ground round the hustings, and of the Upper Market Place, in front. Soon after, Mr Thomas Sheppard, attended by a very considerable number (perhaps about five hundred) of supporters, none of them with sticks or weapons of any sort, entered the Lower Market Place. [We have enquired most particularly, and we find that a request was made by Messrs. Sheppard that not one weapon or stick should be carried by the persons in their procession.] A large party of men, both foot and horse, wearing white colours, then moved from the hustings to meet them; and those who preceded Mr Sheppard's carriage were stopped, and driven back by this party, who formed across the road; and Mr Thomas Sheppard's men being driven to the left, and the contest being on that side, Mr Thomas Sheppard's postillions took advantage of that circumstance, and drove on the right up to the hustings. Mr. Thomas Sheppard and his friends near him were then assaulted by some of the other party, who opposed his entrance to the hustings, and tore part of his and some of his friends' coats from off their backs.

With great difficulty Mr T. Sheppard and several of his friends ascended the hustings, and the business proceeded. Mr Bunn, of Frome, nominated Mr T Sheppard, and was seconded by Mr John Sinkins. Mr Hawkes, of Frome, nominated Sir Thomas Champneys, and was seconded by Mr Jonathan Drew.

On Mr Thomas Sheppard's attempting to speak to the meeting, his voice was drowned by clamour; and, during the whole day, he was unable to obtain a hearing; stones and other missiles were also thrown at him.

Sir Thomas Champneys then addressed the Assembly at great length, and was loudly cheered by his party, and not interrupted by Mr Thomas Sheppard or his party.

Violent and unprovoked attacks were made beneath the hustings, and in other places, on the friends of Mr Thomas Sheppard, several times during the morning.

One poor inoffensive man, Thomas Ford, who offered no provocation, and whose only crime was that he was a friend to Mr Sheppard, was used so brutally that be died on the Thursday following. And so much violence was shewn by the riotous party, that a requisition was made to the magistrates to swear in special constables, to preserve the peace of the town. Captain Edgell, RN of Standerwick-Court, and the Reverend George Rous, Rector of Laverton, magistrates of the Division of Frome, commenced swearing in Special Constables, at the George Inn, at six o'clock in the evening.

Shortly after, a numerous and formidable mob of men with white colours, many of whom were recognized as the men who attended Sir Thomas Champneys, on his entry, armed with cudgels, bludgeons, and stones, without having received any provocation by the magistrates or special constables, forced their way into the George Inn and made an attack on the magistrates and constables.

After a very severe conflict, which continued more than an hour, and in which several on both sides were very seriously wounded, and the inn much damaged, the assailants were driven out, and the door strongly barricaded: but the threats, as well as the conduct of the Rioters were so formidable, that the magistrates sent for a troop of the Seventh Regiment of Dragoons, stationed at Trowbridge, who arrived most promptly that night.

In the mean while the inn was beset by the mob, who deliberately broke the windows, and excluded any public communication with the persons within. During this and the following days an attack on Mr George Sheppard's house being apprehended, three hundred men were kept by Mr G. Sheppard at his house, at Fromefield; and also about two hundred men divided between Mr Byard Sheppard's and Mr William Sheppard's houses, and at their different factories,– these men, after

Monday morning, never going to the Market-Place, or interfering with what was going on there, or in any degree with the election, otherwise than guarding these buildings, except about fifty who were sworn in special constables.

The next morning (Tuesday) the military marched out of town to Beckington, with orders to remain there during the polling, and to return when the poll was closed. – The men were mounted and about to move off, when Sir Thomas Champneys arrived. The polling was adjourned for an hour, that the military might be quite removed before it began.

The polling then commenced, and Sir Thomas Champneys' voters went to the polling-room, from Cork-Street, through the Market-House, which the room adjoined; and Mr Thomas Sheppard's voters went, at first, through the George Inn front door, but about eleven o'clock being interrupted from going that way, went by a private way through the Crown Inn, and a sort of cellar of the George.

About noon, an attempt was made by the mob to force an entrance into the George Inn, which was resolutely resisted by the special constables; several of them suffered from the bludgeons and stones of the assailants. The George Inn front door was now again barricaded.

Many more of the inhabitants of Frome were sworn in as special constables during this morning. Mr T Sheppard did not appear on this day at the hustings or in the town, as his friends and the magistrates wished to prevent any cause of additional excitement in the mob.

On this as well as on the preceding day, many of Mr Thomas Sheppard's supporters were, without provocation, attacked and ill-treated by the bludgeon men wearing white colours, and in the evening the windows of several others of Mr Thomas Sheppard's supporters were demolished, and some of their houses much injured externally and internally.

A little more than an hour after the polling was over, the Dragoons again entered the Town, and remained until about half an hour before the Polling commenced on the next day.

Before the polling commenced on Wednesday, Captain Edgell, one of the magistrates, stated at the hustings to Sir Thomas Champneys, that some of the special constables were armed with firearms, and that, if such violence took place as on the preceding days, they would be ordered by the magistrates to fire.

On the Wednesday, Mr T Sheppard, at the request of the magistrates and his friends, again abstained from appearing in the town. By about ten o'clock, on this day, Mr Thomas Sheppard had polled 163 Votes, which were more than half of the whole number of persons having votes; so that Sir Thomas Champneys, even if he should have polled every other voter, could not have been returned. Indeed, the original number on the List of Voters being 333, and many having, since the list was printed and before the election, been struck off from change of residence and other causes; the number of 163 was considerably above half. At about eleven o'clock, the mob commenced deliberately pelting at the remaining windows of the George Inn; and continued doing so for an hour or two.

Between one and two o'clock pm a large body of the mob wearing white ribbons and favours, (many of whom were recognized as the same men who attended Sir Thomas Champneys' entry,) and shouting,' 'Champneys for Ever,' made a most furious attack on the Crown Inn, (through which, and the George Inn, Mr Sheppard's voters passed to the place where the poll was taken,) for the purpose, it is supposed, of forcing their way into the George Inn, which having been barricaded since the attack on the preceding day, could only be approached this way.

The mob effected an entrance; and proceeded to demolish the bar: one of the special constables had his arm broken, and others were most seriously injured, in attempting to oppose them. The magistrates then ordered the special constables, about twelve of whom were armed with carbines, to make a sally from the George through the Crown and repel the assailants. They succeeded in driving them from the Crown, and in clearing the space in front of that Inn, and of the George as far as the hustings. The magistrates read the Riot Act, and were both struck with stones; and seeing that the mob closed again upon the special constables as they returned, and continued to assail them most violently with stones and brick-bats (some of which were thrown from the hustings,) and that many were already seriously wounded, ordered them to fire. The special constables, many of whom were bleeding profusely from the wounds received from the missiles, determined to preserve coolness and self-forbearance, still remained patient under the showers of missiles which were striking them. They retreated to the Crown door, where they were again attacked by the mob in the same manner. At length, after repeated warnings to the mob of the consequences of their conduct, and earnest entreaties that they would disperse, three or four shots were fired. By these shots two men were severely wounded, one of them below the knee, whose leg it was found necessary to amputate, and the other in the thigh. These two men had taken an active part in the riots: we are happy to find that they are both likely to recover.

The Troop of the Seventh Dragoons, who on the previous day had marched to Beckington, were recalled, and entered the town about three o'clock, which necessarily stopped the poll.

Shortly after the firing Sir Thomas Champneys went home, and in the evening sent in his resignation to the returning officer, requiring that the poll should be opened *pro forma* on the following morning, giving notice that such resignation was without prejudice to any proceedings he might institute as to the election being illegal. The poll was opened on the Thursday, but no votes were tendered; and at the close of the poll the numbers were as follows:

Mr T Sheppard.... 168 Sir T Champneys ...100 —— Majority for Mr Sheppard.... 63

This narrative must not be concluded without congratulating all the respectable portion of the inhabitants of Frome, on possessing in their neighbourhood two such magistrates as Captain Edgell and the Rev Mr Rous, who, during the whole of these three most disgraceful days, shewed unremitting attention to the duties of their station.

It should be also mentioned respecting the two other Magistrates of this division, that one of them, the Earl of Cork, was in Ireland, and the other, the Rev Mr Sainsbury, of Beckington, confined by illness. The Rev F Doveton, of Mells, a magistrate of the division of Mells and Leigh, came to Frome and assisted on Wednesday, and remained until Friday.

To the judicious arrangements of these worthy magistrates, and to the manner in which they were carried into effect, the Borough of Frome owes its escape from a devastation similar to that of Bristol. – And by these measures, even the infuriated mob were saved from the carnage which must have ensued, if it had become necessary to prevent their outrages by means of the military.

JA Wickham, Thomas Bunn, GM. George, JC Yeatman, F Allen, James Edwards, John Harrold, Henry Brittain, George Walters, JW Little, W

NARRATIVE OF FROME RIOT, December, 1832.

We, the undersigned, declare that we have investigated the Facts stated in the following Narrative, and that we believe it to be true.

The Nomination of Candidates for Representing the new Borough of Frome was holden on Monday the 10th. of December instant.

About nine o'clock in the Morning about forty men on foot, bearing Mr. SHEPPARD'S Favors, and without Weapons of any sort, came to Cork Street; and stood quietly near, but not on the Steps of the Hustings, to protect the approach to them.

Sir THOMAS S. M. CHAMPNEYS, Bart. arrived at Half-past Ten, accompanied by many hundred Men and Boys, many of them armed with Bludgeons and Cudgels: most of them were on foot, but they were attended by Men on horseback. A great number of them wore White Ribbons, White Sashes, or Cards inscribed with Sir THOMAS CHAMPNEYS' name; many of them appeared not to be Men of Frome; some of their Bludgeons and Cudgels were loaded with lead.

Some of this Party immediately assailed Mr. T. SHEPPARD'S Men, and drove them away from the Hustings. The Men wearing White Colours, then took possession of the ground round the Hustings, and of the Upper Market Place, in front.

Soon after, Mr. THOMAS SHEPPARD, attended by a very considerable number (perhaps about five hundred) of supporters, none of them with Sticks or Weapons of any sort, entered the Lower Market Place. [We have enquired most particularly, and we find that a request was made by Messrs. SHEPPARD that not one Weapon or Stick should be carried by the persons in their procession.] A large party of Men, both foot and horse, wearing White Colours, then moved from the Hustings to meet them; and those who preceded Mr. SHEPPARD'S Carriage were stopped, and driven back by this Party, who formed across the road; and Mr. THOMAS SHEPPARD'S Men being driven to the left, and the contest being on that side, Mr. THOMAS SHEPPARD'S Postillions took advantage of that circumstance, and drove on the right up to the Hustings. Mr. THOMAS SHEPPARD and his Friends near him were then assaulted by some of the other party, who opposed his entrance to the Hustings, and tore part of his and some of his Friends' Coats from off their Backs.

With great difficulty Mr. T. SHEPPARD and several of his Friends ascended the Hustings, and the business proceeded.

Mr. BUNN, of Frome, nominated Mr. T. SHEPPARD, and was seconded by Mr. JOHN SINKINS. Mr. HAWKER, of Frome, nominated Sir THOMAS CHAMPNEYS, and was seconded by Mr. JONATHAN DREW.

On Mr. THOMAS SHEPPARD'S attempting to speak to the Meeting, his voice was drowned by clamour; and, during the whole day, he was unable to obtain a hearing; stones and other missiles were also thrown at him.

Sir THOMAS CHAMPNEYS then addressed the Assembly at great length, and was loudly cheered by his party, and not interrupted by Mr. THOMAS SHEPPARD or his Party

Violent and unprovoked attacks were made beneath the Hustings, and in other places, on the Friends of Mr. THOMAS SHEPPARD, several times during the Morning.

One poor inoffensive Man, THOMAS FORD, who offered no provocation, and whose only crime was that he was a Friend to Mr. SHEPPARD, was used so brutally that he died on the Thursday following. And so much violence was shewn by the riotous party, that a Requisition was made to the Magistrates to swear in Special Constables, to preserve the peace of the Town.

Captain EDGELL, R.N. of Standerwick-Court, and the Reverend GEORGE ROUS, Rector of Laverton, Magistrates of the Division of Frome, commenced swearing in Special Constables, at the George Inn, at Six o'clock in the Evening.

Shortly after, a numerous and formidable Mob of Men with White Colours, many of whom were recognized as the Men who attended Sir THOMAS CHAMPNEYS, on his Entry, armed with Cudgels, Bludgeons, and Stones, without having received any provocation by the Magistrates or Special Constables, forced their way into the George Inn and made an attack on the Magistrates and Constables.

After a very severe conflict, which continued more than an hour, and in which several on both sides were very seriously wounded, and the Inn much damaged, the assailants were driven out, and the Door strongly barricaded: but the Threats, as well as the Conduct of the Rioters were so formidable, that the Magistrates sent for a Troop of the Seventh Regiment of Dragoons, stationed at Trowbridge, who arrived most promptly that Night.

In the mean while the Inn was beset by the Mob, who deliberately broke the Windows, and excluded any public communication with the Persons within.

During this and the following days an attack on Mr. GEORGE SHEPPARD'S House being apprehended, three hundred Men were kept by Mr. G. SHEPPARD at his House, at Frome-Field; and also about two hundred Men divided between Mr. BYARD SHEPPARD'S and Mr. WILLIAM SHEPPARD'S Houses, and at their different Factories,—these Men, after Monday Morning, never going to the Market-Place, or interfering with what was going on there, or in any degree with the Election, otherwise than guarding these Buildings, except about fifty who were sworn in Special Constables.

The next Morning (Tuesday) the Military marched out of Town to Beckington, with orders to remain there during the Polling, and to return when the Poll was closed.—The Men were Mounted and about to move off, when Sir THOMAS CHAMPNEYS arrived.

The Polling was adjourned for an hour, that the Military might be quite removed before it began.

The Polling then commenced, and Sir THOMAS CHAMPNEYS' Voters went to the Polling-Room, from Cork-Street, through the Market-House, which the Room adjoined; and Mr. THOMAS SHEPPARD'S Voters went, at first, through the George Inn front door, but about Eleven o'clock being interrupted from going that way, went by a Private Way through the Crown Inn, and a sort of Cellar of the George.

About noon, an attempt was made by the Mob to force an entrance into the George Inn, which was resolutely resisted by the Special Constables; several of them suffered from the Bludgeons and Stones of the Assailants. The George Inn front Door was now again barricaded.

Many more of the Inhabitants of Frome were sworn in as Special Constables during this Morning.

Mr. T. SHEPPARD did not appear on this day at the Hustings or in the Town, as his Friends and the Magistrates wished to prevent any cause of additional excitement in the Mob.

On this as well as on the preceding day, many of Mr. Thomas Sheppard's Supporters were, without provocation, attacked and ill treated by the Bludgeon Men wearing White Colors, and in the Evening the Windows of several others of Mr. THOMAS SHEPPARD'S Supporters were demolished, and some of their Houses much injured externally and internally.

A little more than an hour after the Polling was over, the Dragoons again entered the Town, and remained until about half an hour before the Polling commenced on the next day.

Before the Polling commenced on Wednesday, Captain EDGELL, one of the Magistrates, stated on the Hustings to Sir THOMAS CHAMPNEYS, that some of the Special Constables were armed with Fire-Arms, and that, if such Violence took place as on the preceding days, they would be ordered by the Magistrates to Fire.

On the Wednesday, Mr. T. Sheppard, at the request of the Magistrates and his Friends, again abstained from appearing in the Town. By about ten o'clock, on this day, Mr. Thomas Sheppard had Polled 163 Votes, which were more than half of the whole number of Persons having Votes; so that Sir Thomas Champneys, even if he should have Polled every other Voter, could not have been returned. Indeed the original number on the List of Voters being 322, and many having, since the List was Printed and before the Election, been struck off from change of Residence and other causes; the number of 163 was considerably above half. At about Eleven o'clock, the Mob commenced deliberately pelting at the remaining Windows of the George Inn; and continued doing so for an hour or two.

Between one and two o'clock P. M. a large body of the Mob wearing White Ribbons and Favours, (many of whom were recognized as the same Men who attended Sir Thomas Champneys' entry,) and shouting, 'Champney for ever,' made a most furious attack on the Crown Inn, (through which, and the George Inn, Mr. Sheppard's Voters passed to the place where the Poll was taken,) for the purpose, it is supposed, of forcing their way into the George Inn, which having been barricaded since the attack on the preceding day, could only be approached this way.

The Mob effected an entrance; and proceeded to demolish the Bar: one of the Special Constables had his arm broken, and others were most seriously injured, in attempting to oppose them. The Magistrates then ordered the Special Constables, about twelve of whom were armed with Carbines, to make a sally from the George through the Crown and repel the assailants. They succeeded in driving them from the Crown, and in clearing the space in front of that Inn, and of the George as far as the Hustings. The Magistrates read the Riot Act, and were both struck with stones; and seeing that the Mob closed again upon the Special Constables as they returned, and continued to assail them most violently with stones and brick-bats (some of which were thrown from the Hustings,) and that many were already seriously wounded, ordered them to fire. The Special Constables, many of whom were bleeding profusely from the wounds received from the Missiles, determined to preserve coolness and self-forbearance, still remained patient under the showers of Missiles which were striking them. They retreated to the Crown door, where they were again attacked by the Mob in the same manner. At length, after repeated warnings to the Mob of the consequences of their conduct, and earnest entreaties that they would disperse, three or four shots were fired. By these shots two men were severely wounded, one of them below the knee, whose leg it was found necessary to amputate, and the other in the thigh. These two men had taken an active part in the Riots: we are happy to find that they are both likely to recover.

The Troop of the Seventh Dragoons, who on the previous day had marched to Beckington, were recalled, and entered the Town about Three o'clock, which necessarily stopped the Poll.

Shortly after the firing, Sir THOMAS CHAMPNEYS went home, and in the Evening sent in his Resignation to the Returning Officer, requiring that the Poll should be opened *pro forma* on the following Morning, giving Notice that such Resignation was without prejudice to any proceedings he might institute as to the Election being illegal.

The Poll was opened on the Thursday, but no Votes were tendered; and at the Close of the Poll the Numbers were as follow:—

Mr. T. SHEPPARD....163
Sir T. CHAMPNEYS ..100

Majority for Mr. SHEPPARD....63

This Narrative must not be concluded without congratulating all the respectable portion of the Inhabitants of Frome, on possessing in their Neighbourhood two such Magistrates as Captain EDGELL and the Rev. Mr. ROUS, who, during the whole of these three most disgraceful Days, shewed unremitting attention to the Duties of their Station.

It should be also mentioned respecting the two other Magistrates of this Division, that one of them, the EARL OF CORK, was in Ireland, and the other, the Rev. Mr. SAINSBURY, of Beckington, confined by Illness.

The Rev. F. DOVETON, of Mells, a Magistrate of the Division of Mells and Leigh, came to Frome and assisted on Wednesday, and remained until Friday.

To the judicious arrangements of these worthy Magistrates, and to the manner in which they were carried into effect, the Borough of Frome owes its escape from a Devastation similar to that of Bristol.—And, by these Measures, even the infuriated Mob were saved from the Carnage which must have ensued, if it had become necessary to prevent their Outrages by Means of the Military.

Frome, 22nd. December, 1832.

J. A Wickham,	James Baller,	William Giles,	Daniel Bennett,
Thomas Bunn,	Geo. Messiter	Edmund D. Wickham,	Richard Major,
G. M. George,	Daniel Trotman,	Samuel Porter,	W. P. Penny,
J. C. Yeatman,	Harry Hams,	Edward Cockey,	James Holliday,
F. Allen,	Alfred Harrold,	George Allen,	Thomas West,
James Edwards,	Joseph Hopkins,	James Kenwood,	George H. Means,
John Harrold,	Samuel Trotman,	William Hams,	Christopher Moreby,
Henry Brittain,	Samuel Gregory,	Henry Nicholls,	Richard Strong,
George Walters,	Thomas Charles,	James Hill,	L. Perman,
J. W. Little,	John Bridgman,	William Brown,	Samuel Hodder,
W. Nias,	Thomas Pitt,	Thomas Scudamore	J. Plaister,
J. Dommett,	E. G. Pitt,	William Harrold,	R. Deacon,
John Sinkins,	Henry Hillier, Jun.	J. V. Buckler,	Henry Dudden,
Charles Oldfield,	H. Cruse,	Thomas Cruse,	John Hennings,
John Rossiter,	Jacob Player,	John Nicholls, jun.	J. Gregory,
William Cockey,	Lewis Coward,	John Guyer,	Robert Hiscocks,
Henry Rotton,	Barlow Slade,	Elisha King,	John Olive,
W. Rossiter,	J. W. D. Wickham,	G. S. Ward,	Francis Bush,
Edmund Gregory,	W. M. H. Williams,	T. R. Ward,	Francis John Bush.

PENNY, PRINTER AND BOOKSELLER, FROME.

Nias, J Dommett, John Sinkins, Charles Oldfield, John Rossiter, William Cockey, Henry Rotton, W Rossiter, Edmund Gregory, James Baller, Geo. Messiter, Daniel Trotman, Harry Hams, Alfred Harrold, Joseph Hopkins, Samuel Trotman, Samuel Gregory, Thomas Charles, John

Bridgman, Thomas Pitt, EG Pitt, Henry Hilliar, Jun., H Cruse, Jacob Player, Lewis Coward, Barlow Slade, JWD Wickham, WMH. Williams, William Giles, Edmund D Wickham, Samuel Porter, Edward Cockey, George Allen, James Kenwood, William Hams, Henry Nicholls, James Hill, William Brown, Thomas Scudamore, William Harrold, JVBuckler, Thomas Cruse, John Nicholls, jun. John Guyer, Elisha King, GS Ward, TR Ward, Daniel Bennett, Richard Major, WP Penny, James Holliday, Thomas West, George H. Meares, Christopher Moresby, Richard Strong, L Perman, Samuel Hodder, J Plaister, R Deacon, Henry Dudden, John Hunnings J Gregory, Robert Hiscocks, John Olive, Francis Bush, Francis John Bush.

An article in the *Bath and Cheltenham Gazette* gives more details. The correspondent states that the coat was torn from William Sheppard's back as he approached the husting with about 600 supporters from the clothing factories. William was a family member who seems to have acted as an election agent for Thomas. After being introduced by his sponsors Sheppard attempted a speech but was drowned out by the crowd and withdrew.

He (Sheppard) 'was not refused the right of being heard although his speeches had hardly any reference to the occasion, being directed personally as well as generally against those who failed to honour him with their support. During these harangues a party attacked every person who wore the colours of Mr Shepherd, tore down his banners and broke the poles into bludgeons with which they assailed all they suspected to be on the opposite side. These insults were endured till Sir Thomas left hustings and returned to Orchardleigh. A large portion of his violent advocates accompanied him but night brought their return.

Thomas Bunn recorded his experience of going to vote,

... the mob arranged themselves on each side of a long street to pelt all who did not approve of their favourite candidate. I...distained to put a printed paper in front of my hat, to shew them for whom I should vote. The consequence was that I was pelted going and returning from the hustings and the missiles struck me on the back part of my head.[4]

The *Gazette* report continues,

> By this time the magistrates had met at the George Inn and were swearing in special constables. Inspired by this and armed with heavy staves a body of ruffians rushed along the passage of the inn, forced their way upstairs and at length reached the door of the room where the magistrates and constables were deliberating destroying everything and knocking down everyone that came in their way. Here they were met by a few spirited young men who in the absence of constable's staves grasped fire irons, candlesticks and fragments of chairs and with these the lawless gang were beaten along the passage into the stairs, the railings of which furnished other weapons for the constables in the free use of which the wretched assailants were driven into the street. The Dragoon guards arrived and that terminated the first day of electioneering in the new borough.'
>
> On the following day, 11 December, Sir Thomas with his attendants as yesterday entered the marketplace. The appearance of the mob was most frightful, malice and revenge were depicted in every countenance, as the numbers increased their murmurs at length broke out into cries for blood...... While the soldiers were present they abstained from actual violence but on their retiring to the distance from the town required by law on these occasions their vengeance could no longer be suppressed. The friends of Mr Shepherd had collected in the George Inn through which they passed into the polling place under the protection of the magistrates and constables. A strong party of the rioters rushed again into the wide passage but at the risk of danger and life the intrepid constables literally thrashed them back again into the crowd and returned some with broken heads others with mutilated faces. The doors of the inn were then closed and barricaded from within which resisted repeated attempts of the infuriated mob to break them open and the fiends in human shape were left to rectify their malignancy against the windows and freestone front of the inn. At length the storm exhausted itself and the poll proceeded. At the end of the day, Sir Thomas cheered his friends with assurances of triumph thanking them for their faithful and affectionate attachment to him, complimented them on their peaceful demeanour throughout

the day and hoped they would assemble early on the next morning as numerous and conduct themselves as orderly and as quietly as they had on the present occasion. In quitting the town Sir Thomas took with him the usual rabble who in going and returning demolished the windows of every person supposed to be unfriendly to their cause. The devastation in this way which in a short time made rapid progress was stopped early in the evening by the reappearance of the military and the prompt and fearless operation of the civil force. The night was quiet but vengeance was still breathing'.

On the final day Wednesday, 12 December Sir Thomas appeared at the usual hour with his former attendants, both ways which Mr Shepherd's friends had approached the polling place on the former day were now obstructed. They therefore passed through an adjoining house (The Crown Inn) by which they were able to reach it unmolested. Unfortunately, this expedient was soon discovered by a certain Chief of the Rioters who immediately directed a furious number to the door. The scene then became tremendous. It was found necessary to read the riot act as had repeatedly been done the day before and the constables again appeared with the magistrates at their head; 14 of them were now armed with carbines the rest followed with staves and in a few minutes, they showed themselves to the raving mob who challenged them in the most daring manner and assailed them with sticks stones pattens and every missile that could be obtained. Many of the constables were dreadfully wounded. At length Captain Edgell one of the magistrates who had already apprised Sir Thomas of the means of defence in his power again addressed him and begged him to take off the mob, declaring at the same time that responsibility of the consequences would fall upon him if he did not. The safety of the town at length urged that endurance should cease and the magistrates uttered the word *Fire! Fire!* Three carbines were discharged and two of the rioters fell one having lost a leg the other with a ball in his thigh. The report of the carbines struck instant terror into the heart of the mob. Their hands paralysed with fear let fall their formidable sticks and bludgeons which presently strewed the marketplace. The cowards running every direction and Sir Thomas made his departure'.

To the cool discretion of the magistrates and the bravery of our police – to the union which cemented the respectable tradesmen and inhabitants generally the town of Frome is unspeakably indebted. The conduct of the

> magistrates especially is above all praise. They have preserved us from a repetition of the tragedy so lately acted that a not far distant town. We regret to add that two persons are dead, one of the rioters and one of Mr Shepherd's men who is a part of the mob over took in his way home to Chapmanslade and kicked about after they had knocked him down...

On the Thursday morning the polls re-opened but there were no more votes and to his apparent astonishment Champneys lost the election to Sheppard by a majority of 63, 100 votes to 163. The Dragoons were recalled for the night once more and Sir Thomas left to return to Orchardleigh with a large party of followers.

Despite the hatred and violence, it seems that the affair was not without its humorous side. In a letter to the *Somerset Standard* in 1925 following an article on the events a man recalled his father telling the following story: – 'The rival candidates were standing on the balcony of the George to deliver their addresses. Mr Sheppard was not a fluent speaker and had his speech written out and placed in his hat which he held in front of him and read off his speech from it. Sir Thomas Champneys saw what was going on and called out to the crowd, "Gentlemen you must not let your honourable candidate stand bare headed in this inclement weather – beg him to put on his hat" The people shouted "Put on your hat!" and when this was done the flow of eloquence was dammed at the source'. It was also noted that Sheppard wore his hair in a pigtail a style that had fallen from fashion many years before.

Early that evening a Thomas Ford of Short Street near Chapmanslade a weaver and possibly an employee of Mr Sheppard was so badly beaten by the mob that he died of a 'bursting of the small intestine' on the following Thursday.[5] On Saturday 29 December Sir Thomas issued a statement from Orchardleigh having just read his rival's account of events, but it was uncharacteristically short, there was to be no book this time, no comical poem or charges of libel in the civil court. Champneys described *The Narrative* as '...a tissue of concocted falsehoods and low bred autobiography'. He does not have a lot to say but takes issue with a couple of points. The men accompanying him on the day of nomination were some of his tenants, some neighbouring yeomanry and burgesses of Frome who had '...unsolicited, paid me the compliment to breakfast at Orchardleigh'.[6]

He numbers his attendant supporters as '... at least 5,000 who congregated in the most orderly and joyous manner'. and states that once the trouble started he spoke to Captain Edgell and they agreed to appeal to the crowd for calm and for them to 'refrain from any outrage, (Edgell also stated that as for breaking windows, we must always expect that in a contested election)'. Sir Thomas states that he asked those carrying sticks and staves to give them up and that they agreed instantly to this only to be attacked by infuriated 'constables' who commenced hostilities. He admits that stones were thrown from the George but only by 'skulking villains' amongst those already inside and goes on to say that he was 'deliberately levelled at by two ruffians from below with loaded muskets one of which flashed in the pan and was again re-cocked and re-presented and from the musket of the other which was fired in a more elevated position, I now possess the bullet, which was flattened by the wall against which it struck'.

Champneys also claims that the man who was attacked and died on his way home, Mr Ford, was not a friend or supporter of Mr Sheppard as had been claimed but merely someone who had worked at their clothing factory more than two and a half years ago. He finishes his short note with the following flourishes,

> Been put forth to form a shield, as many of the names attached to it (The Narrative) vainly imagine, to their wanton blood thirsty operations on Wednesday, which drove me from a position where with one pointed finger and three words of exhortation, (even hoarse and exhausted as I was) enabled me to lead 10,000 persons to the confines of the town where I took my leave but at parting formed a resolution that I never would again expose myself to the comments of ungrateful, mischief-minded men by showing that forbearance which emanated from my heart and has been so completely thrown away upon the set who have signed this narrative..

The *Narrative* was signed by almost 80 people who declared that '...we have investigated the facts stated in the following narrative and we believe it to be true...' Near the top of the list was the name 'George Messiter' followed by at least eight people from the church vestry list who had sided with Rev Ireland in the great sexton debate of 24 years before and a number of other family names that match. Doubtless there would have been more had not the intervening 24 years taken its toll. Further evidence of a feud going back decades if not generations. Was the anti-Champneys camp made up of those to whom the family had long owed money? There is not enough surviving evidence to provide an answer but there is a lot more to this story than would appear at first glance. There are two sides to every story and then there's the truth.

[1] Gill p 34
[2] Public Ledger 1832-05-23
[3] *Narrative of the Frome Riot* December 1832 copy in Frome Museum but re-typed here with unnecessary capitalisation removed and some spellings adjusted.
[4] Gill p 34
[5] Coroner's Inquest at the Black Dog Standerwick. *Devizes Gazette*
[6] *Somerset Standard* reprinted 1925-01-13 'To the worthy inhabitants at large of the parish of Frome and its vicinity'.

15
THE AFTERMATH. TAUNTON MARCH 1833

On 3 March 1833 the trial of those arrested during the election riots opened. James Wheeler, Richard Hill, Joseph Stokes, Henry Gregory, Joseph Short and Samuel Button were charged with 'riotous assembly with divers others and assaulting two constables in the execution of their duty'. Charges of 'maliciously shouting' against four other men were dropped.

The Rev George Rous was the first prosecution witness, he was a local magistrate and rector of Laverton and set the scene as outlined in the preceding chapter. He explained that by the Tuesday morning about 200 special constables had been selected and were subject to a hail of stones with many badly injured. Amongst those involved with the swearing in was solicitor George Messiter who, the witness agreed, 'is not friendly with Sir Thomas Champneys'. Twelve of the constables had been armed with carbines and formed a line outside the George, the Riot Act was read from the porch of the pub but the stones kept coming and despite repeated warnings the mob would not disperse, so the order was given to fire, which four or five did but only once. They were instructed to aim low and pick out the most active, two persons were shot, one had his leg amputated and the other was still in hospital at the time of the trial. The prisoners had been in custody since the following Thursday as bail was refused. Defence counsel implied during cross examination that the constables were all Sheppard's supporters but Rous stated that he did not know this to be the case and that line of questioning was stopped by the judge.

One of the next called was William Giles, a special constable. He saw Hill and Stokes at the head of the mob threaten the constables with sticks and was himself 'severely wounded in the face with a stone'. Henry

Gregory was there with a white ribbon but no stick. Giles continues: – 'The mob could not attack us directly because of our bayonets, Mr Rous said, "Gentlemen you must fire! four shots were fired. I did not fire".' One unnamed constable claimed that so few shots were fired because the carbines of some of the men were too damaged by the stones to fire properly. 'After the shooting Sir Thomas's carriage was ordered and he went off most of the mob accompanying him. I voted for Mr Sheppard.'

Joseph Oxley, a cooper and maltster was next. He saw Gregory daring the constables to fire at him, and said that his windows and doors were broken and his family were driven out of their house by the mob.

Henry Britten, a surgeon, was a special constable who saw Gregory at the head of a mob of 20-30 people and addressing them. He levelled his piece at Gregory but did not fire. He saw Stokes at the Crown door with a bludgeon in his hand and strike a man three of four blows to the head. 'I was very much wounded and spent three days in bed. My little finger was broken', he claimed.

Joseph Hague was a special constable who was hit by Stokes and was senseless for four days. Francis Bush gave corroborative evidence to say that Hague's life was in danger for three or four days. He also claimed during cross-examination that he had known Gregory since he was a child and described him as 'an industrious hard working and honest man. He is a baker and pork butcher in a considerable line of business beyond his beer house'.

James Clement Parker, special constable saw Hill, Stokes and Wheeler with bludgeons challenging the constables to a fight and Wheeler was smashing windows. Daniel Bennett a local wine merchant, saw James Wheeler smashing windows.

Thomas West stated that, 'I saw Hill at the Angel Inn and heard him say to the landlord, 'Mr White if you suffer those troops to remain in your house tonight your house shall come down'.

George Messiter, solicitor and magistrates clerk, saw Hill and Short waving sticks and making a noise. Richard Major gave evidence that, 'Gregory pointed me out to the mob and said, "That is one of Sheppard's party," and they beat me with sticks'. Elisha King and other witnesses saw 'many persons' go into Gregory's yard and collect sticks.

Henry Nicholls, aged 19, one of the special constables, saw Button and Stokes breaking windows and stated that 'I had a carbine on the

Wednesday and levelled my gun at Carpenter who was throwing stones and shot him'.

The defence case was very short and consisted of a few witnesses stating that they had seen Gregory stop people from removing sticks from his yard and that his wife had had a lock put on the door. Defence counsel made the point that the first magistrate to be called for the swearing in of the constables 'entered the inn of the Sheppard party' and contended that, 'if constables had been called in on both sides there would have been no riot'.

Despite strong evidence of bias, the jury convicted all the defendants who were sentenced to eight months hard labour with Gregory bound over in his own recognisance for the sum of £50 to keep the peace for two years.

There the matter ended but a few points emerge. Tribal loyalties were obviously very deep and of long standing amongst the populace with the political policies of the parties hardly relevant. Sir Thomas had a large amount of personal charisma, he was a good speaker and attracted a fierce loyalty amongst the lower orders – a fascination and even respect often seen between the highest and the lowest in society united against the pious and self-righteous middle orders. Above all it must be remembered that all his often-fanatical followers had no vote; the 300 or so that did were of the middle class, the same class as Sheppard – shopkeepers, bankers, solicitors, and manufacturers and property owners, and like attracts like. To this class antagonism may be added personal disputes going back decades, and it is surprising that Champneys achieved as many votes as he did – had the seething mob been enfranchised the result may have been very different.

Champney's election disappointment was to be as nothing compared to the coming events of 1834/35.

16
TAUNTON ASSIZES, APRIL 1834

THE CASE OF *Wright and Co. Bankers and Another v Levy*, a sheriff's officer to whom Sir Thomas had become indebted was held before Mr Baron Williams on Friday 4 April 1834.

This matter was referred from the King's Bench to try the question as to the right of Levy to take goods belonging to Champneys after they had been assigned by a bill of sale to Wright and Co. to whom he owed almost £6,000. The details of the claim are of little interest, being a squabble over who had first claim on the contents of Orchardleigh, but the evidence does give us an insight into Sir Thomas's affairs. There are no surviving transcripts of the case and so we are reliant on newspaper reports which can be a little stilted. One interesting fact is that Lady Champneys was not living at Orchardleigh during this time but was preparing to move back in once the loan had been agreed; presumably she was with family in Wales. It was also stated that Sir Thomas was in occupation of Orchardleigh until June 1833 and his servants remained until October. The fine carriage that he had used during his election campaign was now replaced by a pony and trap.

In December 1831 Sir Thomas obtained a loan of £30,000 from the Norwich Union to be drawn on the bank, Wright and Co. of Covent Garden. The deal was brokered by a William Youens and at first, they were very reluctant, as Sir Thomas had recently been released from prison for debts totalling £250,000 but Youens explained that Lady Champneys had just inherited an annual income of £11,000 from her father's estate plus some property and that repayments could easily be made from the remainder of Sir Thomas's rental income. Unfortunately, 'Sir Thomas's necessities compelled him to apply these to other purposes...' Youens told the court. Matters were made much more difficult as the new Lord

Mostyn and other members of Lady Champneys family contested the will so that the promised money was tied up in court; she won eventually but not until November 1834.

Unsurprisingly Champneys failed to keep up the payments and the bank pressed for their money but none was forthcoming. After several letters requesting payment were ignored the bank sent their clerk out to Orchardleigh and met Sir Thomas and Youens, after a stormy meeting during which Sir Thomas said that he had no money, had 'not expected such treatment' and threatened to find another bank to take his account. Youens took Sir Thomas into another room and calmed him down getting him to see that as he had nothing more to secure the loan against he must accept the bank's terms.

They obtained a 'bill of sale' over the contents of Orchardleigh which meant that a borrower would transfer ownership of their goods as security for a loan to the lender but keep possession of them while making repayments. Once the loan was repaid the borrower would regain ownership. This move also entitled the lender to put a man on the premises to take an inventory and even live there to make sure that the goods were not sold on or otherwise disposed of. Sir Thomas suggested that one of his own stewards could fulfil this role – a suggestion that was not taken up – and Thomas Ivey the sheriff's officer of Frome was put in place. All this was taking place while Sir Thomas was canvassing for the Frome election and he objected strongly to anyone from the town being involved, as word would get around and injure his chances. Champneys made such strong objections to Ivey sleeping at his house that a deal was struck whereby Ivey would turn up every day instead. An inventory was taken and the bill of sale was put in place on 1 November 1832 with the proviso that no sale would take place for three weeks during which time Ivey maintained control of the entire contents of Orchardleigh. There were other creditors with claims circling the estate and Ivey's job involved keeping these at bay as much as it did preventing the owner from removing goods. After so many seizures of the contents at Orchardleigh it is a surprise that there was anything left, but some of the furniture was described on the sales particulars as 'little used' so the presumption must surely be that as the bailiffs removed one set furniture through the front door so Champneys obtained replacements on credit and in through the back door.

Sir Thomas's fears about the small Frome electorate finding out about his situation were well founded but unavoidable, as at least two of his creditors were on the voting list themselves. One Frome resident who would have taken great delight in the situation was Henry Miller, solicitor and election agent for Sheppard. He was owed money and had taken some silver plate and 40 or 50 bottles of wine from Orchardleigh to cover the debt in April of 1833. As part of the election banter there was apparently a 'squib', as the various pamphlets were called which referred to a 'branch of ivy being placed at Orchardleigh'.

The verdict was for Wright and Co the plaintiffs. A couple of weeks later there was an application by Mr Sergeant Bompas on behalf of Levy for a new trial on the grounds that the judge had mis-directed the jury.

Yet again no money was forthcoming and with Sir Thomas still in prison on Wednesday 21 May and Thursday 22 Messers English and Fasana sold without the least reserve 'An Assemblage of Fashionable and Valuable Furniture. Cellar of Fine Old Wines several Valuable Paintings and Prints. A Grand Piano-forte etc'. at their rooms in Milsom Street, Bath.

No sooner had one auction ended than another started. The next one was run by Messrs. Farebrother and Co. of The Strand, London and was to take place on three successive days from 27 July 1835 at Orchardleigh House itself. The lots included household furniture, books, bed linen, horses and even plants and plant pots. There was a collection of pictures amongst which was *The Infant Friends* by Sir Joshua Reynolds.

In the end the George was chosen for the auction as Champneys refused to have it at Orchardleigh. Thomas Green a local businessman went through some of the lots which he said aroused enormous interest and sold well and he bid on an antique ebony cabinet and some curtains for which he paid 90/- after estimating their cost as £30-£40.[2]

On Saturday 8 August 1835 Sir Thomas and his steward Robert White appeared at the Court for the Relief of Insolvent Debtors sitting at the Court House, Winchester in an appeal for their release from prison. Both were described as late of Orchardleigh Park and Hayling Island near Portsmouth. No one appeared to oppose the appeal and they were both released but not without some harsh and revealing words from the judge. White was alleged to be in debt for the sum of around £14,000 chiefly 'acceptances on behalf of his employer', Sir Thomas. He was

SALE of FURNITURE, extensive Wardrobe of BED and TABLE LINEN, WINES, &c.

UNDER AN EXECUTION BY THE SHERIFF,

The Property of Sir T. S. MOSTYN CHAMPNEYS, Bart.

Messrs. ENGLISH and FASANA

Beg to make known that they will

SELL BY AUCTION,

WITHOUT THE LEAST RESERVE AND EXEMPT FROM DUTY,

This present THURSDAY, May 22, and following day, at Twelve o'Clock,

AN Assemblage of Fashionable and Valuable FURNITURE, Cellar of fine OLD WINES, a few valuable PICTURES, Macklin's Bible, splendid copy; Bed and Table LINEN, Grand PIANO-FORTE; iron Garden Roller, 30 diameter; an Otaheite Canoe, a Boat, &c.; which has been removed from Orchardleigh Park, to

Their Rooms, Milsom-Street, Bath,

FOR THE GREATER FACILITY OF SALE.

The Furniture is of the best description and but little used, and comprises a set of ten oak gothic chairs, covered in crimson cloth and gold lace; beautiful marqueterie cabinet and commode, sets of solid rosewood chairs, with sofa, card and occasional tables to suit; handsome Brussels carpets; a magnificent glass, single plate, 71 in. by 49; a pair of richly gilt consol tables, with real Verde-antique tops; set of mahogany dinner tables; three-tier side tables; also the furniture of the wood lodge; magnificent OR-MOLU CLOCK, and several lots of prime bedding and chamber furniture.

Also, a Cellar of most excellent OLD WINES, chiefly Claret, Madeira, Sherry, Bucellas, and Port, all purchased from London merchants, regardless of expense. Upwards of 130 dozen of wine bottles, and numerous miscellaneous articles.

May be viewed the morning of sale. Catalogues are ready. Samples of the wines will be produced at the time of sale.

Bath Chronicle 15 May 1834

about 24 years of age and as there was no opposition he was discharged with the admonition to be more circumspect in future.

Next came the turn of Sir Thomas whose release was also unopposed. It appeared that he had received a discharge in the insolvent court building in Taunton in October 1827. From that time until the death of Sir Thomas Mostyn in 1831 he had been 'living on the bounty of his friends', sometimes receiving £100 or £200 at a time. On a review of the schedule it appeared that his debts amounted to around £84,000. The first 122 named creditors were described as disputed or doubtful and discounted. Several questions were put as to the manner in which the debts were contracted and we begin to get a picture of his extravagance.

Messrs Houlditch of 93 Longacre were creditors for £1,200 for debts contracted previous to his discharge in 1827 for a carriage and a loan of carriages as well as an advance in money the exact amount of which was uncertain as he was in the habit of writing his name on blank acceptances. Mr Robinson an upholsterer of Curzon Street, Mayfair, was owed £750 for furniture sent to the house and another upholsterer Mr Thomas Taylor of new Bond Street was owed £437 for the same thing.

There were various other amounts of a similar nature as well as £350 for plate sent to Orchardleigh Park where it remained about 15 months unopened having 'by fraudulent claims fallen into the hands by Mr Lazarus by whom he (Champneys), declared he had been robbed to a considerable amount'. Some of the purchases of plate and furniture had been made on account of the expected early return of Lady Champneys to Orchardleigh Park. Previous to discharging the insolvent the Commissioner addressed him 'as one of considerable experience in pecuniary difficulties and strongly admonished him on impropriety, however embarrassing his circumstances of taking into service young men scarcely emerged from boyhood, inducing them to enter on a career of experiments instead of labouring upwards in the path of usefulness and honourable exertion'. The baronet declared in response, and with the greatest fervour, that he was innocent of inducing Robert White to attach his name to acceptances, but that his signature was obtained through the intervention of one of his agents. 'Sir Thomas was evidently labouring under severe indisposition and appeared acutely to feel his present situation especially when alluding to the result of the sale at Orchardleigh Park which took place at the commencement of the week'.

Presumably he returned to an empty mansion at Orchardleigh a broken man, 66 years of age and in failing health – but he had not lost all of his fight; as the remaining years went by there were complaining letters to the partners at his uncle's firm Cox and Co. the freehold owners of Orchardleigh. People were coming and shooting game without offering any to the family, and the cutting of timber went on apace. In 1833 there was a letter from Cox's local agent saying that young people had been apprehended for stealing firewood and was it was not worthwhile taking them to court as after the reform bill it was unlikely that the offenders would be transported.[2]

Nor had he lost his love of print; -

To the Editor of the *Salisbury and Winchester Journal* 24 August 1835
Sir, In passing through Salisbury, on my road to Orchardleigh from Winchester, I found upon my breakfast table at the Antelope Hotel, *The Globe* newspaper of Monday last in which a long and laboured detail appears respecting certain occurrences which took place before Mr Commissioner Reynolds at Winchester on the 7th inst. and detailed by the Hampshire newspaper of the 10th, to the editor of which journal a fruitless application was made on the 11th to insert the *real facts* of the case and thereby administer an antidote to the mischievous and cruel bane they had promulgated.

In justice, therefore to myself and the those excellent and feeling minds who have expressed themselves deeply interested in my sufferings, I consider it a duty to intrude upon your columns with the request that you will permit me to state in the first instance, that as the multiplicity of extraneous questions put by the 'learned and impartial' Commissioner were all answered by himself and closed by a sermonic lecture on the *Follies of the Day* there was no opportunity for explanation on the more important points of examining the balance of assets to meet every claim, (124 of which number are now re-entered as disputed under the veto of the court) any more than a permission given to me to show that I had been plundered by one individual in 18 months to the enormous extent of the upwards of £53,000 and how poignant and cruel had been my sufferings and persecutions, at the head of which must ever stand the wicked plunder of Orchardleigh House upon which it was a poor consolation to be told by the court that the parties engaged therein must refund the value of the property *before the sale.*

I should regret to appear an egotist or in the most remote degree push myself before the public; but, thrust upon their notice as I have mischievously been at this time, I feel that I am only doing my duty,

I am Sir respectfully,
THOMAS MOSTYN CHAMPNEYS
Salisbury August 19th 1835.

[1] McGarvie, M. *Eighty Years of Frome.* Frome UDC 1974
[2] Jones p.25

17
A SURFEIT OF MAGNIFICENCE

SIR THOMAS DIED on 21 November 1839 and it is said that he was buried in a special coffin which had been on display in the undertakers shop window in Frome Market Place for some days.[1] The house in which he died was only a few yards from the church but he had eight bearers, each one presented with a new suit for the occasion and the payment of a guinea. He was buried like his forebears in the small church of St Mary at Orchardleigh.

Thomas certainly received a bad press during and after his lifetime; how much of it was deserved or down to prejudice and rivalry we don't know, but a good case can be made out for history having misjudged him. He certainly inherited the family trait of being reckless with money, which being born into enormous debt he did nothing to quell. But despite having many enemies who were more than ready to spread, or maybe create, stories about his sexual preferences, he does not seem to have had a reputation for drinking or gambling, which was attached to the lost fortunes of so many of his class, although he was undoubtedly vain, boastful, quick to take offence and arrogant. Despite his faults he was regarded with some affection among the lower orders, probably due to his fairness as a magistrate, his epitaph reads,

> Sacred to the memory of Sir Thomas Swymmer Mostyn Champneys. Bart., who departed this life 21 November 1839 in the 71st year of his age. Sir Thomas was the 25th in lineal descent from the first possessor of Orchardleigh and the 23rd from Sir Amian Champneys and his wife the Lady Anne Courteney granddaughter maternally of Louis, King of France. The late baronet filled the office of High Sheriff of Somersetshire

in 1800, with great magnificence; was Deputy Lieutenant, and for many years a most active and popular Magistrate of the County, and through life was an unostentatious and liberal friend to the poor.

Thomas Bunn, who was one of the signatories of *The Narrative* and certainly not a fan, comments on his death in his diary: -

With most of the advantages which providence confers on human beings, he contrived to make himself despised and detested, and passed many years in gaol. His person and his beautiful residence were avoided like a pestilence except by a few of the most degraded of his species. Yet to give every man his due. In the middle of his pecuniary distress he sent us several hundred pounds to purchase the leasehold interest of two acres of ground now forming the site and burial ground of Christ Church...which no other person was inclined to supply.

In his gay [*sic*], days I understand he drove six fine horses in his carriage, since which he passed several years in prison. He lately, in the last extremity of illness applied to me for the loan of a wheelchair which I keep for invalids. He wrote me a jocose letter not on his own infirmities but on those of the wheelchair. He is said to have died £100,000 in debt but left directions for a sumptuous funeral. [2]

Sheppard stood for election again in 1835 and retained his seat by a majority of four, it being reported that it had cost him £10,000 in bribes to achieve this.[3] Having long renounced his progressive stance he stood as a candidate for the Conservative Party and remained in the Commons until he retired in 1847 at the age of 81.

Lady Charlotte Champneys, Sir Thomas's wife, died in 1845, much respected for having paid off a great number of the family debts amounting to about £30,000, and the church bells in Frome were rung to express their gratitude to her. It is unfortunate that her voice is completely silent throughout the whole of the story and that, despite her staying with him amidst all his troubles, we have no clue to the true nature of their relationship or her opinion on how Champneys ran his affairs. As mentioned before marriages amongst the aristocracy were much akin to business and property dealings rather than affairs of the heart, and under the rules at that time there would have been no

A stone pillar marks all that remains of the ancestral home of the Champneys, demolished in 1860

way out of the marriage for Charlotte other than by proving adultery – assuming that she was unhappy with her appointed role. There were no children and so the baronetcy and the family line ended with her, but the name lives on as a large shopping development in Llandudno – 'Mostyn Champneys Retail Park' and, appropriately enough, a small cul de sac in Frome. For a family with such a long history and a man of such vanity it is inconcievable that there are no family portraits, but apart from the one from childhood already noted it seems that none have survived, or that they were widely dispersed during the many house sales and sit unprovenanced in galleries or private collections. Any personal mementoes or family papers seem to have been dispersed or lost and even the ancient house itself demolished.

Orchardleigh Park and House became the property of Sir Thomas's uncle Richard Henry Cox, receiver in bankruptcy, who put it all up for auction in 1855, an auction that had been planned since 1849. The estate was bought by William Duckworth who tore down the old house once his new one was completed in a rather awkward jumble of styles that was fashionable at the time. The estate remained in that family until the 1980s when it was divided up and sold in lots with the Duckworth's house becoming a fashionable wedding venue and golf course.

[1] Jones 1969 p24 and YB9 p61
[2].Gill. *Experiences of a 19c Gentleman.* FSLS. 2003
[3].Belham, P. *The Making of Frome* 1973

APPENDIX

This article first appeared in the *Frome Yearbook* issue 24, 2021

SHAKESPEARE'S NIGHT IN FROME? AN 18TH-CENTURY MYSTERY

In 1806 John Deacon the sexton of St. John's church in Frome died and the vicar, William Ireland, took it upon himself to appoint Deacon's son Robert in his place. This was taken as an act of provocation by Thomas Swymmer Champneys, master of Orchardleigh, whose family had, as lords of the manor, held the right of appointment for many generations. Champneys had his own man for the position, Richard Champneys Soane, who was probably the illegitimate son of his grandfather Richard and battle lines were drawn.

Ireland and Champneys had been enemies for some time and had been in dispute over rents and landownership for a number of years. Ireland, who kept a mistress not far from his church, has been described as greedy, gluttonous and hypocritical, and Champneys as 'vain, arrogant and stupid'. Champneys had many admirers amongst the lower orders of the neighbourhood who saw his judgements as a magistrate as fair and just. He was, however, heartily disliked by the professional establishment within the town. Neither side was to give way on the appointment which was quite lucrative, involving certain rights and powers, and when Soane arrived for work in November 1806 he found the doors barred and entry denied.

The matter went to court in June 1807 and resulted in an outright win for Soane and Champneys. Ireland refused to accept the decision and tried to prove that Champneys had no right to the Orchardleigh estate and therefore no right to appoint the sexton. The case went back to court, the previous judgement was confirmed, Soane was duly installed and there the matter would have ended were it not for the character of the victor.

Thomas Champneys was a difficult and complex man. His family claimed to have come over with William of Normandy in 1066 and claimed to have owned the Orchardleigh estates and others since late medieval times. Their income was derived in the main from rents and sugar plantations in Jamaica but the family's fortunes had taken a serious turn for the worst many years before and Thomas had been born into huge debt. His strategy for dealing with this was to bury his head in the sand until confronted with bailiffs or court orders, at which time he would borrow more money to cover previous debts, all the while spending outrageously on parties, balls, court cases and building projects.

His response to the victory over Ireland was typical – a childish bout of gleeful gloating, triumphalism and name calling. In 1808 he produced a book, *The Hieromania*[1] which translates roughly, as 'the mania of priests' It was a 54-page 127 stanza poem, humorous, obscure and surreal in equal measure. The work was unsigned and its preface was addressed to 'The Worthy and Respectable Inhabitants of F[rome]'. It purports to be the story of a man from that town telling his story from the condemned cell. His situation arose from an 'early indulgence' in such venial crimes as robbing orchards, smuggling, unlawfully destroying game and poaching. His skills were always much in demand by local gangs with whom he poached from Longleat, Mells and Orchardleigh, amongst other estates. The imaginary author and felon owed an 'inveterate grudge' against the 'intrepid magistrate of O[rchardleigh]' who had often frustrated his villainy and while in prison awaiting the hangman he penned the poem *Hieromania* and passed it to his editor, along with a five-pound note to pay for its publication.

Champneys' book was intended for a limited audience who would have recognised themselves and others named only by initials and was distributed amongst the local gentry, clergy and well-to-do of the Frome area. Its general flavour can be seen from Stanza 21 in which the author comments upon one of Ireland's visits to Orchardleigh,

Has't thou then O[rchardleigh] forgot,
It's wine, its fatted haunch?

When at my table thou wert wont
To cram thy monstrous paunch.

The work contains many footnotes that enable the 'editor' to pay tribute to the 'author', particularly when the latter praises the noble line of Champneys or comes up with a particularly clever phrase; both are of course, Tom Champneys himself. One of these footnotes explains the author's use of the term 'blueskin' in his poem and refers to a document that he had seen and copied out because it mentioned his home town of Frome.

From *The Hieromania* p.14 stanza 10
The lawless Blueskin* gang of F(rome)
Rebellow'd loud his voice,
And echoing back their parson's oath,
Swore to oppose the choice.

*"Blueskin"-- In a manuscript journal amongst various other fragments said to have been written by Shakespear, Anne Hathaway and other contemporary writers, which I remember to have seen, I was much struck with the following item, and being a man of F(rome) copied it:

"October 12mo, 1583, Sent by mie fatherre to Wayell faire, with our nayborne coombe; in oure waye backe, lodged a nighte att F(rome), wheare mie fellow travialler had delinges in the clothe waye. I noted the people seemed of the race of the Pictes, theire skines being blew, by the constant use of that sort of coller; but what I marvelled much att theire lippes, even those of theire woomen have moore of the lillie than the roase , and from a tricke on twoo plaied me during my sojourne theare, I much feare mee theire hartes are as blacke as theire lippes are white, and that one is a proofe of the other.---"

This item in the great dramatist's journal induces me to think that when he uses the expression "lily livered" as he does in Macbeth:

"Go prick thy face, and over- red thy cheek",
"Thou lily livered boy!"

> He refers to the lips, and not the liver, and that the real expression is "lily levered," that is pale lipped, which, ever after the F(rome) adventure, Shakespear always considered that criterion, not only of a cowardly, but of a black heart.
> Note by Ho****t.

Champneys is not attempting to prove that Shakespeare visited Frome, which gives weight to the idea that he believed what he saw to be genuine. He has no particular interest in Shakespeare or whether he spent the night in Frome; he is merely trying to explain his own use of the word 'blueskin'. He makes no note of where or when he saw this document, again underlining its lack of importance to him. It would not have been within his own family archives as there would have been no need to copy it. He refers to it as a 'journal' and the entry starts with a date as though it was a diary. There is also some doubt that he saw the document himself as the footnote is signed 'Note by Ho****t.' which is less than helpful. Is this Champneys himself under yet another pseudonym or is it another 'man of Frome'?

Is it really credible that Shakespeare visited Frome in 1583 and spent the night there with his wife and child? The footnote consists of 103 words attributed to Shakespeare.

Very little is known about his life before 1592, but it is known that he and his wife Anne Hathaway had their first child, Susanna, christened on 26 May 1583 when William was about 19.

As for the substance of the note, the word *Nayborne,* presumably means 'newborn', as the child would have been about five to six months old at the time of the supposed visit. The following word '*coombe*' is odd as it is normally taken to mean valley but this maybe a mis-transcription.

The note states that he was sent by his father John to *Wayell* Fair which is almost certainly Weyhill near Andover about 100 miles from Stratford and 40 miles from Frome. Frome is far from a direct route back to Stratford and the little party must have had a good reason for going there. The fair was one of England's oldest and most important medieval fairs, which took place three times in the year, April for trading cattle, July for selling lambs and October for hops. Amongst other things it was one of the largest sheep fairs in the country, trading up to 100,000

A portrait dating from 1606, and said to be Shakespeare

sheep a day at its height. Cheeses were brought from the counties of Wiltshire, Somerset and Gloucestershire. Hawkers selling all manner of trinkets and entertainers of all kinds would have taken advantage of the visitors. Gambling on the outcome of dog and cock fighting and bear baiting was common and duels and jousts were held. With stalls for the traders, pens for the animals, food stalls and inns, permanent and tented structures, it would have been a crowded and exhilarating place which grew to such an extent, that by the sixteenth century a court was established there to deal with disputes.

The note continues that on their way back they *lodged a nighte att F(rome), wheare mie fellow travialler had delinges in the clothe waye*. Who is the fellow traveller with dealings in the cloth trade? Were they buying wool at the fair to sell to a dealer in Frome, a well-known wool town, or were the two visits unconnected?

William's father John was a glovemaker who was also known to have been a dealer in illegal wool and hides, as well as deriving income from a number of property deals, rentals and money lending. It is also known that he travelled as far as London in search of wool when it was in short supply. The family fortunes took a drastic turn for the worse in the late 1570s and William is thought to have left school in about 1578 when he was 14 to help the family out of dire circumstances. The exact details are unknown but much property was sold off and John was subject to some heavy fines which he seemed unable to pay.

By 1583 things became very bad for John Shakespeare and his circle who were Catholics, or at least part of a group of sympathisers. Elizabeth I was in great fear of Popish plots and initiated a campaign against known sympathisers. Throughout the autumn of 1583 the atmosphere in the household at Henley Street, Stratford on Avon must have been one of increasing paranoia. On 25 October John Somerville from a village not far from Stratford was arrested at an inn on the way to London where he declared that he was off to assassinate the queen. He was probably mentally ill and the plot sprung purely from his own imagination, but his father in law was Edward Arden – the head of Shakespeare's mother's family and a prominent catholic. Real or not Somerville's actions were enough to lead to an armed raid on Arden's house and the arrest of his family. The 'plot' was linked to others, and a general round up of Catholics ensued with many accused of treason. Arden and others were executed that November; whether the house in Henley Street was raided we do not know but it was certainly a very dangerous time and it would not be unreasonable for John to have sent the young family out of harm's way if he feared an attack by government forces was imminent.

As well as a centre for wool Frome was famous for a particular blue dye made from *Isatis tinctoria* or the woad plant, the very same plant used by the ancient Britons to colour their bodies, and which stained the hands and bodies of those working in the dyeing industry in Frome.[3] So far everything in the footnote rings true but then the note describes the lips as being *moore of the lilliee than the roase,* the implication being that work in the dyeing trade had also caused a whitening of the lips, something not recorded elsewhere. And what was the *tricke or twoo plaid me during my sojourne theare* which turned him so against the townsfolk? Was it just that they were overcharged at the inn? Unfortunately, he does not elaborate and that is all that is recorded of William Shakespeare's time in Frome.

Champneys adds an observation of his own concerning the term *lily-livered* which he re-interprets as meaning lily-lipped (*lily levered*) which would fit in with what he believed to be Shakespeare's observation in the footnote. In this he is almost certainly mistaken. The first known mention of 'lily livered' comes from Macbeth in around 1605. In medieval times the liver was thought to have been the seat of the emotions, and to be lily coloured was to be bloodless and cowardly. When Shakespeare was writing, the prevailing belief was that there were four bodily fluids, or *humours,* whose balance affected health and character. Those with too much blood were *sanguine,* cheerful or courageous. A person with an overabundance of black bile was *melancholy* (or sad); a person with too much phlegm was *phlegmatic* (or unexcitable); too much yellow bile was *choleric* (or aggressive and hot-tempered). It was also possible to have too little of one of these humours; medieval physicians believed that yellow bile was produced in the liver, and the liver of someone who produced too little of this bile would be pale. Since yellow bile is associated with a warlike, aggressive disposition, a person with a deficiency of it would be weak and cowardly. Taking what he believes to be Shakespeare's meaning Champneys combines this cowardly disposition with an evil intent, or black heart.

Returning to Frome in 1808, the recipients of *Hieromania* were outraged at the way they were portrayed and demanded revenge. Champneys had not signed the book and all that could be done was to arrest the printer, the hapless John MacDonald, for libel. He received six months in Marshalsea prison for his troubles but refused to name the author.[3]

Despite the facts fitting the little we know about the 'lost period' of Shakespeare's life and the possibility that he really did visit Frome there is an alternative possibility.

WILLIAM HENRY IRELAND 1775-1835 [2]

IN THE MID eighteenth-century Shakespeare was largely neglected outside London, and in 1769 actor/managers David Garrick and Charles Macklin hit upon the idea of a Shakespeare Jubilee to be held over three days in the bard's birthplace to make some money and

William Henry Ireland at the time of the forgeries

publicise the bard. No one seemed to mind or notice that this was five years after the actual anniversary of his birth in 1564 and the event was very well attended despite almost continuous rain over the entire three days. The event caused the birth of an industry. Sensing that there was money to be made those locals indifferent or unaware of William Shakespeare became world experts and Stratford was suddenly full of articles and souvenirs from his life. More artefacts were made and sold from a mulberry tree supposedly planted by Shakespeare than pieces of the true cross in medieval times. Stratford became a place of pilgrimage and the faithful turned up in droves seeking anything connected with the playwright, but what they wanted more than anything were documents written or signed by Shakespeare himself and of this there remained not a scrap. Chief among those to see the opportunities in this burgeoning market was John Jordan, a wheelwright turned poet and now self-appointed keeper of the bard's legacy and guide to all things Shakespearean.

Prominent among the Shakespeare fanatics of the time was Samuel Ireland a London artist, engraver and book collector, who had been a friend of Garrick and who visited Stratford in the summer of 1793 seeking out Jordon in the hope that he would help to track down some original manuscripts. With Samuel was his 'slow witted' son William Henry Ireland. The gullible pair were led a merry dance to the extent of being introduced to an old gentleman who had been in receipt of a large bundle of parchments 'signed and to do with Shakespeare' but who had burned them all a few weeks before to make room for some partridges. Samuel believed every word of this heartless joke and returned to London broken hearted. These events in Stratford deeply affected young William.

Family life in the Ireland household at 8 Norfolk Street near The Strand was rather unconventional even for the time. Samuel lived with a woman named Freeman, a former mistress of Lord Sandwich – officially Samuel's housekeeper, but in fact his mistress. The rest of the family comprised William and his two sisters. The parentage of any of the children is a matter of speculation, which concerns us here only because the lack of certainty had a lifelong effect upon William. Samuel hinted at a dark secret to do with his parentage but the truth was never explained to him. William was brought up amongst London's theatreland which he loved at the expense of more conventional studies, leading his masters to believe that he was 'incorrigibly stupid'. Home life consisted of nightly readings and enactments of the works of Shakespeare with William constantly at pains to win the approval of his disinterested father; then, as now, the best that could be done for such a hopeless case was an apprenticeship to the law and so it proved.

Stuck in the conveyancer's office with little to do the 17-year-old began to dream. One of the lad's heroes was Thomas Chatterton, a child genius from Bristol who fooled the artistic world by convincing them that he had found some original documents by a medieval poet named Thomas Rowley. They were brilliant forgeries but overcome by poverty, depression and lack of recognition Chatterton killed himself in 1770 at the age of 17. Seeking to emulate his hero and impress his father, William was determined to produce the one thing that Samuel desired more than anything else, a document signed by Shakespeare.

On 16 December 1794 he announced to Samuel that he had met a gentleman of means who had a large chest of old documents that were of no interest to him. Permitted to ferret about and take whatever he wanted, and to William's intense astonishment, one of the first things to attract his attention was a mortgage deed bearing the signature *William Shakespeare* – the very thing that his distant father had said he would give his library to possess! Samuel showed it with pride to his friends and fellow collectors who pronounced it genuine. Samuel was determined to meet the benefactor and see what else the trunk might contain but, unfortunately, William had sworn an oath never to reveal the man's identity. Overcome by such unaccustomed praise and attention William declared that he had seen even more of Shakespeare's manuscripts in the chest and he would bring them to Samuel.

Experts of the day came to Norfolk Street and exclaimed their delight at the genuineness of the ever-increasing pile of documents undoubtedly from the hand of the bard. William was both flattered and amazed and from there the matter escalated... He produced an original manuscript of King Lear but with all the rude bits removed – this, exclaimed the experts was the true Shakespeare with the ribaldry having been introduced by others at a later date. It was quite common for theatre producers to adapt plays as they saw fit – even Garrick had done so. There were no surviving copies of Shakespeare's manuscripts –

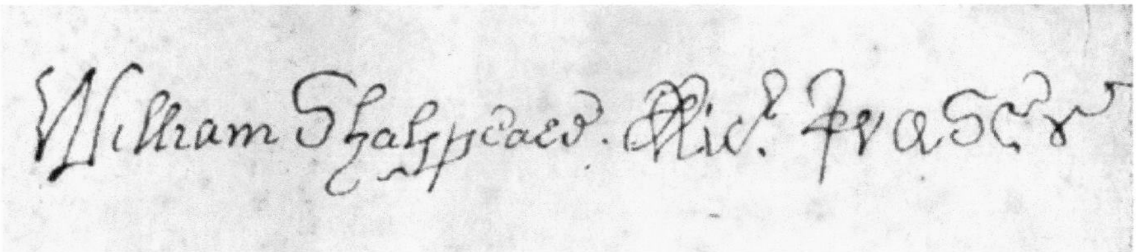

One of Ireland's forgeries of Shakespeare's signature

not a single line and no copyright restrictions – the play and its wording belonged to whoever was producing the work at the time and this they tailored to suit their audience which could be more akin to a football or pub crowd than today.

The more the experts authenticated William's documents the bolder he became, surely he was now the equal of Shakespeare, in fact his versions were *preferred*! He continued to produce documents from the mystery chest one of which proved to be a declaration of loyalty to Queen Elizabeth and the protestant religion, a 'Profession of Faith' dispelling for all time the rumours that Shakespeare had catholic sympathies – to the absolute delight of his gullible audience. William was now bringing home antique books from Shakespeare's private library annotated by the bard himself. All this had been produced in a matter of weeks from the end of 1794 to the beginning of 1795.

In February of 1795 Samuel decided that his collection was extensive enough to parade before the world and opened his house at 8 Norfolk Street to the learned and fashionable amongst whom we might guess was Thomas Champneys on one of his visits to the capital. James Boswell was invited around to give an opinion and after taking his time to examine every aspect of the documents set before him, declared that he would die contented having seen these relics; and indeed, he did, dying three months later and before the deception was exposed.

The Shakespeare experts who had authenticated the manuscripts had only seen them briefly under Samuel's watchful eye. They were satisfied as to the date of the vellum, type of ink used and style of handwriting, which appeared to be of the right period. There was nothing else to go on as there were no known samples of Shakespeare's handwriting with which to compare these documents. None of them had had an opportunity for prolonged study and the range of Shakespeare adaptations and alterations was so large that judgement on artistic grounds alone was not really possible from such small samples – if at all.

All this was about to change. Pressured by his father's passion for acquisition William's output changed from the barely credible to outright farce. When a friend mentioned that should a descendent of Shakespeare's emerge he might have a claim to the entire estate William returned to the chest once more and discovered a 'Deed of Gift' by Shakespeare which left some of his plays and documents to a long dead ancestor named, incredibly, William Henry Ireland who had once saved him from drowning.

A scene from Vortigern & Rowena

The situation could not continue. Samuel had decided to publish the entire collection in facsimile without consulting his son. Meanwhile, William discovered the most wonderful item of all – the magical chest had disgorged an unknown Shakespeare play *Vortigern and Rowena*! Despite many suspicions Richard Sheridan who was greatly in debt and had a theatre to fill agreed to stage it, paying Samuel £250 plus one half of the profits. Samuel's book of manuscripts was supposed to have been published after the play was performed but production problems meant that it had still not been performed when the book came out on 24 December 1795. Now that the works could be studied at leisure events took a very different turn.

Edmond Malone, the most celebrated Shakespeare scholar of the time, and one who did not believe in the authenticity of the manuscripts, published a volume consisting of over 400 pages of evidence claiming that all the documents were forgeries. He exposed numerous historical inaccuracies, proof of incorrect handwriting and lists of words that weren't used in Shakespeare's time.

Literary London was divided over their authenticity and the long-awaited play opened on 2 April 1796 at Drury Lane with John Philip Kemble in the lead role. It was not ascribed to Shakespeare, but nonetheless the theatre was packed with more than 3000 people. Kemble had no faith in the work and was playing the whole thing for laughs. There were great outbursts of ridicule and disruption as the performance progressed and there was not to be a second performance.

What had started out as an exercise to please his father was now totally out of control and William realised that the game was up. He confessed all but Samuel refused to believe it, firmly of the opinion that his son was far too stupid to have fooled anyone let alone himself and the leading experts. This must have hurt William deeply but what was worse was that the gossip mongers were assuming that it was Samuel himself who had produced the forgeries. In June of 1796 William Henry left Norfolk Street never to return. Still believing himself to be a genius he moved around borrowing money and began what he hoped would be an artistic career in his own right. By December William had decided to publish a full confession to save his father from further ridicule and might even make some money by cashing in on the scandal that his forgeries had produced. He was 19 years old. The *Authentic Account of the Shakespearian Manuscripts* was published as a 43-page pamphlet and all 500 sold immediately at 1s. He explained how he had found a recipe for old ink, scrounged blank sheets of vellum from documents at work along with ancient seals, and scoured bookshops for items of an appropriate age. Incredibly father Samuel produced a book of his own, *Mr. Ireland's Vindication of His Conduct Respecting the Publication of the Supposed Shakespeare Mss.* a full catalogue of all the documents which he still believed to be authentic. It won him no sympathy and father and son could not be reconciled; they met only once more before Samuel died of diabetes in 1800.

Despite being offered thousands for the manuscripts when belief in them was at its height, the only money they made out of the entire affair was £353 in profits from the single night of the Vortigern play of which William received £90. William married and made a precarious living by accepting orders for new forgeries in Elizabethan script as well as selling numerous copies of what he claimed were *the* original manuscripts of his forgeries to collectors. Could it have been one of these copies that Champneys saw? Which, if any, of the volumes contains the authentic originals is unknown, and perhaps unknowable. All the supposed original manuscripts were different in content and are now spread throughout the world, no comprehensive catalogue has been attempted. The British Library has one version. Is it possible that the only genuine document in Shakespeare's hand is a journal mentioning a trip to Frome? It must be assumed that Champneys had no thought of the document he saw being a fake despite Ireland having confessed some years before. A journal or diary does not appear in any known list of Ireland's creations. What happened to it? Did its owner consign it to the flames once news of the scandal reached him or had he known it was fake but was having a bit of fun at Champneys' expense? He made numerous trips to London for balls and functions where he could have been shown the documents.

Champneys' reference to a document by Anne Hathaway is intriguing as she is generally thought of as being illiterate. It is known that Ireland forged a love letter from Shakespeare to Anne and possibly it was a copy of this that he saw. If it is by Ireland how did he know about Frome and the blue dye? Had he been here himself and been subject to, *a tricke or twoo*, played by the rascally natives? He lived briefly in Bristol during the summer of 1796 so it is possible that he visited Frome but this is slightly after the period of his admitted forgeries.

Amongst the many things that should have led the experts of the time to believe that the documents were forgeries was the outlandish spelling. Ireland added random vowels and consonants throughout his texts and added an 'e' at the end of many words. Although this was a time before formalised spelling some of his creations have no historical precedent. When the words in the footnote are compared to the printed text of Ireland's bogus early version of King Lear, for instance, some are the same – 'Fatherre' for father, and 'feare' for fear; but many are not. The footnote has 'harte' for heart, Lear has hearte, the note has nighte' for night, Lear has nyghte' and throughout Ireland's writings my is spelt mye but the footnote has mie. Edmond Malone in his exposure of the manuscripts pointed out that a good deal of the spelling didn't seem to belong to the period – or any time in recorded history! Champneys' quotation from the supposed journal consists of only 113 words, too few for any meaningful comparison.

The question must remain open. Somewhere in an ancient chest or an unexplored library archive there just might be Shakespeare's journal detailing his early years and visit to Frome or an unrecorded manuscript by the notorious eighteenth-century forger, William Henry Ireland.

[1] Champney's gloating poem *The Hieromania* is freely available on-line via Google books

[2] By far the best book on the whole affair is by Bernard Grebanier. *The Great Shakespeare Forgery* Norton and Co.1965

[3] McGarvie Book of Frome p94 'When the Rev. Richard Warner visited Frome in 1801 he still found the labouring people 'As deeply tinged as Ancient Britons' with the dye'

BIBLIOGRAPHY

An Act for sale of part of the settled estates, late of Richard Champneys squire, deceased for payment of his debts and legacies and for other purposes therein mentioned. (Frome Museum. copied transcript from 1770)

Betham, Revd *The Baronetage of England* (Franklin Classics rpt.1803)

Burke, P. *Celebrated Trials Connected with the Upper Classes of Society*. (Nabu Press rpt.1851)

Champneys, TS. *A Letter to The Right Honourable the Earl Poulett, Lord Lieutenant and Custos Rotulorum of his Majesty's County of Somerset etc.* (Crockers 1804) (SRO Taunton DD\X\TCR/3)

Champneys, TS. *Substance of a speech, delivered by T. S. Champneys, Esq. late Lieut. Colonel Commandant of the Selwood Forest Legion, to the Corps, on his resignation of the command, Monday, March 12th 1804.* Frome, Printed at the desire of the Corps. (Crockers. 1804).

Champneys TS. *Minutes of the Proceedings in the Election of a Sexton* (John Macdonald 1808)

Champneys, TS. *The Hieromania.* (Pegasus Press 1808 and Google Books)

Champneys, TS. *A Narrative of the proceedings with the particulars of the trial at Wells in the month of August 1808 relative to the appointment of a sexton to the parish church of Frome Selwood.* 1809. (Frome Public Library)

Champneys, TS. *Facts attending the prosecution of Thomas Swymmer Champneys one of the magistrates of the County of Somerset for an alleged assault and false imprisonment preferred by Thomas West.* Bristol pub Joseph Routh, Narrow Wine St. 1815.

Champneys, TS. *Letters of Sir Thomas Champneys, bart. imprisoned for debt, respecting his treatment by the Governor.* (1824 SRO Taunton Q/AGI/18/1)

Champneys, TS. *Letter to the Rev Rouse.* (Bath 1828)

Clarke and Co. (publishers) *The Trial of John McDonald, Printer 1814*

Collinson, John. The *History and Antiquities of the County of Somerset.* Volume 2 1791 (Google Books)

Gill, B. *Experiences of a 19c Gentleman.* (Thomas Bunn) (FSLS 2003)

Goodall, R. *The Industries of Frome* (FSLS 2009)

Jones, K.R. *The Cox's ofCraig Court and Hillingdon.* (Frome Museum 1969)

McGarvie, M. *The Book of Frome* (Barracuda Books 1980)

McGarvie, M. *Light in Selwood* (FSLS 1976)

McGarvie, M. *The Mystery of Fidele* (FSLS 1999)

McGarvie, M. *Eighty Years of Frome* (FSLS 1974)

McGarvie, M. *Orchardleigh in the time of the Champneys.* (Dorset Notes and Queries. Sept 1994)

McGarvie, M. *Monumental Inscriptions St Mary's Orchardleigh* (FSYB Vol.2 1988)

McGarvie, M. (ed) *Crime and Punishment in Regency Frome* FSLS 1984

Messiter, G. *Report of the trial of an indictment preferred by Sir Thomas S. Champneys, Bart. against Geo. Messiter, Gent. ... with an appendix containing the baronet's correspondence ...* (George Messiter 1822 and SRO Taunton L56-1 (9)

Norton, R. *Blackmail, The Gay Subculture in Georgian England,* (on-line essay 2009)

Pooll, A.H. *A West Country Potpourri* (Privately Printed 1969)

Richardson, H. *Slander: report of the Trial of George Messiter, Attorney, of Frome Selwood, in Somersetshire, for Gross, Wilful, and Malicious Slander, on Thomas Swymmer Champneys, Esquire* (Redford and Robins 1820. and SRO Taunton Tite 110-10)

Richardson, H. *Report on the trial of George Messiter attorney, Nathanial Messiter woolstapler and banker, and John Messiter their kinsman, for trespass, assault, and false imprisonment upon the person of TS Champneys baronet, and one of his Majesty's justices of the peace for the counties of Somerset and Wiltshire and a deputy lieutenant of the same.*
(Philanthropic Society, St George's Fields. London 1820)

Woodford, James. *Diary of a Country Parson*

INDEX

A'Court, Lady, 28
Abraham, Moses, 79
Alderman & Mrs Gobble, 25
Algar, Rev. J, 77
Amiens, Peace of, 30
Ammerdown, 28
Amport, Hampshire, 17
Antelope Hotel, 151
Arden, Edward, 162
Arnold, Elizabeth, 10,11
Assize Court, Bridgwater, 37, 53, 60, 105
Assize Court, Salisbury, 43, 55, 85
Assize Court, Surrey, 101
Assize Court, Taunton, 22, 65, 103, 109, 117, 121, 143-145, 146-152, 172-173
Assize Court, Wells, 23, 48, 57, 61, 65, 87, 106, 108, 172
Astley, Sir J MP, 102, 112
Atkinson, Thomas, 67
Avery, Benjamin, 6
Azor, 17,19-20,

Baily, Thomas, 47, 48
Bampfylde, Sir Charles, 99
Barter, William, 93
Bath, Lord, 26, 28, 43, 45, 46, 50, 56, 61, 73, 74, 76, 78,
Bathurst, Lord & Lady, 26
Batt, Thomas, 11,
Bayley, Justice, 48, 101
Bayly, William Davis, 77, 113, 122,
Baynton, John & William, 47
Beckford, William, 27, 41, 75
Beckington, 7, 32-35, 110, 133, 135
Bell, The Frome, 92
Biggs, James, 73-74
Black Dog Inn, 82-84, 87-88, 142
Blacksbridge (Blatchbridge), 61
Blueskins, 59, 159, 160
Bowden, Samuel, poet, 6
Boyle, Edmund 8th Earl, 50, 127
Bristol, 6, 7, 9, 63, 112,113,126, 135, 166, 170, 173
Britten, Henry, 144
Broderib, Zachariah, 64-65
Broderip, Edmund & Co., 68
Bruton, 72, 122
Buckingham, Marchioness of, 49
Bunn, Thomas, 19, 20, 47, 77, 98, 130, 131, 135, 137, 154, 173,
Burrough, Mr Justice, 85, 87, 89, 94, 103, 104
Bush, Dr. Francis, 92, 137, 144
Button, Samuel, 143, 144

Camms Hall, 119
Caroline, Queen, 97-99
Cassan, SH, 77
Champneys, Sir Amian, 5, 153
Champneys, Caroline, (sister), 10, 21
Champneys, Caroline Ann (Cox), 8,13, 26, 63
Champneys, Charlotte (Mostyn), 17, 19, 21, 51, 74, 126, 146, 154
Champneys, Henry, 6
Champneys, Sir Hugh, 6
Champneys, Sir John, 6
Champneys, Katherine Chandler, 7
Champneys, Richard, 5, 6-7,9, 12-14, 17, 46-47, 48, 112-113, 157, 172
Champneys, Sarah, (Daines), 6, 113
Champneys, Sir Thomas, 6-9, 12-13, 16, 21
Champneys, Thomas Swymmer, 1-173
Chancery, Court of, 9, 12, 100, 115, 126
Charles I King, 119
Charlotte, Queen, 74, 97, 99
Chatham, Earl of, 50

Chatterton, Thomas, 166
Chislett, William, 63, 81
Christchurch, 78,123
Clarendon Hotel, 101
Clarke, John, gatekeeper, 124
Clarke's River, 112
Cockey, Edward/William, 3, 135, 136
Coldbath Fields, 101
Collinson, John, 1, 4, 173
Cooke, Joseph, 47
Cork, Lord, 21, 28, 50, 53, 56, 73, 77, 78, 127, 135
Corner, William, 37, 64-65, 108
Cox, Caroline Ann, 8, 63
Cox, Richard Henry, 8-9,13, 15, 54, 63, 90, 113, 115, 155, 173
Crocker, Abraham, 21, 23,
Crocker, Edmund, 21, 29
Crook, Mrs, 90
Crosier, Ralph, 64-65, 94
Crown Inn, Frome, 33, 133, 134, 139, 144
Cuzner, John, 87-89, 90, 92, 108

Daines, Sir William, 6,
Davis, Charles, 27
Davis (turnkey), 117-118,
Davis, William, 89, 91
Davis, William Bayly, 77, 113
Deacon, John, 43, 44, 46, 157
Deacon, Robert, 44, 136, 157
Dickson, William, MP, 119
Domesday Book, 1
Drury Lane, 22, 40, 169
Duckworth, Margaret, 20
Duckworth, William, 6, 155, 156
Dupre, Mrs., 41

Eagle, The, 73
Edgell, Captain, 132, 133, 135, 139, 141,
Edgell, James Stephen, tailor, 125
Ellenborough, Lord Chief Justice, 48, 71, 96
English and Fasana auctioneers, 148
Evill, solicitor, 82, 84, 86
Exton, Hampshire, 13, 99

Fareham, Hampshire, 6, 46, 119
Farleigh Hungerford, 37, 38, 39, 40,
Fidele's Grassy Tomb, 20-21, 28, 173
Fisher, Miss Clara, 74
Fitzherbert, Mrs, 26, 40,
Foley House, 26, 40, 50
Fonthill, 75
Ford, Thomas, 132, 140, 141
Fontaine, Elias Benjamin de la, 7,
Frederick, King of Prussia, 17
French, John, clothier, 92
Frome, 1, 2, 3, 6, 10, 12, 13, 15, 18, 27, 30, 31, 32, 34, 35, 37, 43, 44, 47, 48, 55, 56, 57, 58, 61, 62, 71, 73, 74, 76, 77, 79, 80, 81, 82, 83, 84, 85, 86, 88, 89, 91, 92, 93, 97, 98, 99, 109, 110,111, 113, 115, 118,119, 120,121, 122, 123, 125, 127- 142, 147,148,153, 154, 155, 157, 158, 159, 160, 162, 163, 164, 170, 171, 172-173
Frome Infantry, 31, 32, 33, 37, 82, 128
Frome Selwood Troop, 30, 31, 35, 36, 172
Fromefield, 2, 127, 132
Fry, James, 108,
Fry, Robert, 90, 108
Fry, William, 108

Garrick, David, 9, 164, 165, 166,
Gaselee, Stephen, 85, 90, 92, 109
George Hotel, 73, 76, 79, 111, 127, 129, 132, 134, 138, 140, 143 148
George III, King, 22, 26, 49, 53, 74, 98
George IV, King, 26, 97, 98, 127
Giles, John Allen, 80
Giles, William, 136, 143, 144
Glastonbury, Lord, 23,
Globe, The, 151
Gloucester Lodge, 49, 50, 53,
Gloucester, Prince William of, 26, 41, 49, 50
Gore, Lady, 28
Gowen, Simeon, 70
Graham, Baron Justice, 37
Greenland, Stephen, 92

Gregory, Henry, 74, 143-145,
Gregory, Isaac, 62-63, 73, 74,
Grose, Mr. Justice, 38,
Guise, Sir W, 28

Hadfield, James, 22-23,
Hanover Square, London, 9, 17
Hardy, William Erasmus, 117-118
Harrow, School, 10-11, 12, 15, 26
Hart, John Minter, 102-103
Hathaway, Anne, 159, 160, 170
Hawarden, Viscountess, 28
Hawkins, Sir John, 28
Heath, Dr schoolmaster, 10
Hertford, Marchioness of, 41
Hieromania, poem, 46, 55-61, 65, 67, 158-159, 163, 171, 172
Higgins, George, 82, 85, 100, 101, 123-126
Hill, Richard, 143-144
Hillier, landlord, 129
Hindon, 75,
Hinton St George, 32,
Hippisley, Sir John Cox, 28, 93
Hook, Theodore, 118
Horcerlei, 1
Horner, Thomas Strangeways, 37, 56
Horningsham, 43, 44, 93,
Houlton, Robert, 38-40,
Howard and Gibbs, 116
Hulbert, William Henry, 125-126
Hunt, Henry 'Orator', 119-121

Ilchester Jail, 3, 109, 115, 116, 117, 119, 121
Ireland, Alicia, 44, 58, 61, 65
Ireland, Samuel, 165-170
Ireland, Rev.William, 43-54, 55-63, 94, 141, 157, 158
Ireland, William Henry, 164-171
Ivey, Thomas. constable, 83, 84, 85, 115, 147, 148,

Jamaica, 6, 7, 9, 12, 13, 75, 112-113, 158
Javelin men, 21, 22, 24
Jones, Thomas, postmaster, 33
Jordan, John, 165,

Keington, James, 106
Kemble, John Philip, 169
King, George, 105
King, John, 32
King's Bench, 38, 42, 47, 69, 81, 82, 87, 93, 96, 97, 98, 99, 104, 109, 110, 113, 115, 146
Kingdon, George, 63, 67, 98
Kingston, Court, 101, 102, 103, 104
Knatchbull, Charles, 34, 77

Lambert, Lady, 41
Lazarus, Mr, 150
Ledyard, TW, 34
Leeds, Duchess of, 41
Lens, Mr. barrister, 58, 66
Lethbridge, Sir Thomas Buckler, 99, 102, 103, 119, 120
Lewis, J O, 18, 29, 97, 110
Lewis, Noah Edward, 104-105,
Littledale, Mr. Justice, 120
London, 7, 8, 17, 18, 24, 25, 26, 27, 28, 33, 40-41, 49, 50, 55, 72, 75, 77, 82, 90, 96, 98, 99, 102, 103, 105, 106, 108, 109, 115, 116, 117, 127, 128, 130, 148, 162, 164, 169, 170
Lullington, 12, 50, 71, 87, 90, 93, 108
Lyall, George., 128, 129, 130

Maberly, 104,
Macdonald, John, printer, 55, 57, 58, 163, 172
McGrath, Edward, 104,
Malmesbury, Lord, 26,
Malone, Edmond, 169, 171
Manners, Lady Louisa, 26
Market Place, Frome, 33, 90, 120, 127, 129, 130-132, 138-139, 153,
Marlborough, Duchess of, 41
Marshalsea prison, 38, 57, 163
Marston Bigot, 51, 71
Mason, Mr, schoolmaster, 10
Maude, The Hon Mr, 28
Medley, John B Rev., 19
Melbourne, Viscountess, 50

Mells, 37, 55, 56, 73, 123, 135, 158
Merland, Sir Henry de, 5, 52,
Merland, John de, 5
Messiter, George, 56, 70, 80, 82-87, 88-92, 94, 96, 103, 104, 106-111, 120, 121, 135, 141, 143, 144, 173
Messiter, John, 84, 85
Messiter, Nathanial, 30, 82
Middlesex Sessions, 101, 102, 103
Middleton, John, 33
Miller, Henry solicitor, 129, 148
Minutes of the Proceedings.., 55, 56, 57, 172
Mitchell, Sarah, 125
Mold, Flintshire, 13, 16, 112,113,
Morning Post, 27, 41, 75, 111, 118
Mostyn, Charlotte Margaret, 17,
Mostyn, Sir Roger, 17, 53
Mostyn, Sir Thomas, 21, 87, 126, 150
Mount-Norris, Countess of, 27
Mountjoy, Lord, 28

Narrative of the Frome Riot, 56, 58, 130, 135, 140-141, 154, 172
Narrative of the Proceedings... Relative to the appointment of a Sexton... 54, 57
Newbolt, Sir Henry, 20
Newgate Prison, 102, 103
Nicholls, Henry, 137, 144-145
Norfolk Street, London, 165, 166, 167, 169,
Nutts River, Jamaica, 6, 13, 115

Oddy, Thomas, 105
Olive, Edward /John, 3, 32, 37, 137
Orchardleigh, 1, 5, 6, 12, 15, 18, 19, 22, 23, 24, 25, 26, 27, 32, 34, 35, 37, 38, 39, 41, 44, 45, 46, 47, 48, 49, 50, 51, 52, 53, 55, 56, 57, 58, 59, 63, 64, 65, 66, 68, 71, 73, 74, 75, 79, 80, 81, 89, 95, 99, 105, 106, 110,111, 115, 118, 122, 124, 125, 137, 140, 146, 147, 148, 150, 151, 153, 155, 157, 158, 173
Oxley, Joseph, 144

Palmer, Henry, 99, 100, 101, 102, 103
Panford, Richard, 105
Park, Thomas Joshua, 101
Parker, Anthony, gamekeeper, 37
Parker, James Clement, 144
Pell, Serjeant Albert, 58, 85, 87, 88, 92, 94, 106,
Penton Lodge, 16-17, 18
Peterloo, 119
Pole-Carew, Reginald, 34
Poulett, John 4th Earl, 32-35, 42, 172
Power, Lieutenant Colonel, 32
Prince of Wales, 25, 26, 27, 40, 41, 49
Pye, Anthony, 9, 104

Rendlesham, Baron, 25, 50
Representation of the People Act, 127
Richardson, Mr Justice, 106, 109,,
Richardson, Rev Benjamin, 37, 39, 40,
Ridley, Lady, 28
Riots, 30, 71, 135, 143,
Rode, 106
Rogers, Rev John Methuen, 77, 93
Rotch, Benjamin, 102
Rous, Rev George, 132, 135, 143, 144, 172
Ryall & Howard, auctioneers, 118,

Sainsbury, John magistrate, 39, 76, 98, 135
St. Catherine's Chapel, 6
St. James Palace, 12, 27, 49
St. John,, Hon General Frederick, 126,
St. John's Parish Church, 43, 47, 48, 55, 123, 157
St. Mary's Church, Orchardleigh, 5, 6, 13, 19, 21, 111, 153, 173,
Saint Thomas in the East, 112
Saunders, William, 108-109
Scott, Sir George Gilbert, 6
Seaman, Rev Lionel, 47
Selwood Forest Legion, 30, 32, 35, 172
Shakespeare, John, 160, 162
Shakespeare, William, 157-171

Sheppard, Byard, 132
Sheppard, George, 32, 93,127, 132,
Sheppard, John, 6
Sheppard, Thomas, 127, 128-135, 140-141, 143, 144-145, 154
Sheppard, William, 32, 33, 34, 37, 128, 132, 137
Sheridan, Richard, 168,
Sheriff of Somerset, 6, 9, 13, 21, 22-23, 68, 82, 153
Short, Joseph, 143, 144
Sidmouth, Devon, 34
Singer, John Webb, 1, 54, 62, 122
Sion Hill, 41
Skinner, Rev. John, 50, 54
Skurray, Francis, 93
Skurray, Thomas, 7
Slade, James, clothier, 32, 37,
Slavery, 113, 114, 115, 129
Soane / Sone, Richard Champneys, 44, 46,47, 48, 55, 157
Somerville, John, 162
Southampton, 7, 112
Spencer, William, 42
Spring Gardens, Frome, 1, 3,
Standerwick, 82, 132, 142
Star Life Annuity, 116
Stirling, Sir Walter, banker, 117,
Stokes, Joseph, 143, 144
Strangford, Lord, 28
Stuart, Lord, 28
Sugar plantations, 6, 7, 9, 112, 115, 158
Swymmer, Anthony Langley, 7, 8, 13, 112, 122,
Swymmer, Jane Langley, 6, 112,

Tarleton, Lieutenant General, 34-35,
Taunton, 22, 65, 99, 103, 109, 117, 121, 143-152
Thellusson, Elizabeth/Peter, 25, 26, 40, 41, 50
Thornhill, Richard Badham, 37, 38, 39, 64, 72
Thynne, John, 26

Vaslet, Lewis, 10
Vaughan, John and Philip, 113
Vincent, Charles, 88-89, 91,
Vortigern & Rowena, 168, 170

Waggon and Horses, Frome, 12, 88
Wakefield, David, 113
Walker, Mrs, 24
Warminster, 82-83
Wells, 23, 48, 54, 57, 61, 65, 87, 93, 106, 108, 172
West, John, 67-68, 70,71, 94
West, Thomas, 58, 63, 137, 144
Westbury work, 89
Weyhill Fair, 160
Weymouth Arms, Frome, 62
Wheeler, Henry, 90,91
Wheeler, James, 143, 144
White, John. bailiff, 68-69, 71
White, Robert, 148, 150
Wickham, James Anthony, 23, 30, 34, 38, 39, 48, 98, 135, 136
William, Prince of Gloucester, 26, 41, 49, 50
Williams, Justice Baron, 146
Williamson, sheriff, 84
Willoughby, Charles, 89, 91
Winchester College, 12, 112
Woad, 2, 163,
Woodforde, Samuel/James, 18, 28
Wool, 2, 3, 30, 79, 82, 90, 108, 127, 162, 173
Woolverton, 40, 110
Wright & Co, 146, 148

York, Duke of, 26, 37
Youens, William, 146-147